THE INTEGRITY OF
THE PERSONALITY

Also by Anthony Storr

SEXUAL DEVIATION

HUMAN AGGRESSION

THE DYNAMICS OF CREATION

JUNG

THE ART OF PSYCHOTHERAPY

THE ESSENTIAL JUNG
(selected and edited by Anthony Storr)

SOLITUDE: A RETURN TO THE SELF

CHURCHILL'S BLACK DOG, KAFKA'S MICE AND
OTHER PHENOMENA OF THE HUMAN MIND

HUMAN DESTRUCTIVENESS

THE INTEGRITY OF THE PERSONALITY

ANTHONY STORR

BALLANTINE BOOKS NEW YORK

To C.S.

Originally published in Great Britain by William Heinemann Medical
Books Ltd. in 1960.

Library of Congress Catalog Card Number: 91-92254
ISBN: 0-345-37585-8

Text design by Holly Johnson
Cover art: *Land of the Midnight Sun* by Diana Ong (Superstock, Inc.)

Manufactured in the United States of America

First Ballantine Books Edition: January 1992
10 9 8 7 6 5 4 3 2 1

ACKNOWLEDGEMENTS

My thanks are due to the following authors and publishers for permission to use various quotations:

Mr. E. M. Forster and Edward Arnold Ltd for passages from *Howards End* and *Two Cheers for Democracy*.

Dr. A. W. Heim and Methuen & Co. for an extract from *The Appraisal of Intelligence*.

Dr. W. Ronald D. Fairbairn and Tavistock Publications Ltd for several passages from *Psycho-Analytic Studies of the Personality*, and to the same author for extracts from papers published in the *British Journal of Medical Psychology*.

Mr. Leonard Woolf for a quotation from Virginia Woolf's essay "The Patron and the Crocus" in *The Common Reader*.

Messrs. Chatto and Windus for a sentence from *Proper Studies*, by Aldous Huxley; and for two extracts from *Remembrance of Things Past*, by Marcel Proust, translated by C. K. Scott Moncrieff.

The Hogarth Press for extracts from *Outline of Psycho-Analysis* and *New Introductory Lectures on Psycho-Analysis*, by Sigmund Freud.

The Hutchinson Group for a passage from *The Physicist's Conception of Nature*, by W. Heisenberg.

Cassell & Co. for excerpts from *Clinical Psychiatry*, by Mayer-Gross, Slater, and Roth.

The Syndics of the Cambridge University Press for extracts from *The Nature of the Physical World*, by A. S. Eddington, and from *Science and the Modern World*, by A. N. Whitehead.

J. M. Dent and Sons for a passage from Joseph Conrad's *Nostromo*.

Routledge and Kegan Paul for quotations from *The Fear of Freedom*, by Erich Fromm; from *The Interpretation of Nature and the Psyche*, by C. G. Jung and W. Pauli; and from the following works by C. G. Jung: *Psychological Types, Two Essays on Analytical Psychology, Modern Man in Search of a Soul, The Undiscovered Self*, and *The Development of Personality*.

Penguin Books Ltd. for extracts from W. Hamilton's translation of Plato's *Symposium*; and for a passage from *Child Care and the Growth of Love*, by John Bowlby.

Macmillan & Co. for a passage by T. H. Huxley quoted by Aldous Huxley in *T. H. Huxley as a Literary Man*; and for a sentence from *Reality*, by B. H. Streeter.

George Allen and Unwin Ltd. for two quotations from *Introductory Lectures on Psycho-Analysis*, by Sigmund Freud; for extracts from *The Way and Its Power*, by Arthur Waley; and for a sentence from *History of Western Philosophy*, by Bertrand Russell.

Gerald Duckworth & Co. for a passage from *Psycho-Analysis and Politics*, by R. E. Money-Kyrle.

G. Bell & Sons for a quotation from *Christianity and History*, by Herbert Butterfield.

Weidenfeld and Nicolson Ltd. for a passage from *Einstein*, by Antonia Vallentin; and for an extract from *The Greek Experience*, by C. M. Bowra.

Dr. Derek Richter and H. K. Lewis and Co. for a passage from W. R. Ashby's essay, "The Cerebral Mechanisms of Intelligent Action," in *Perspectives in Neuro-psychiatry*.

CONTENTS

FOREWORD

This book was first published by Heinemann Medical Books in 1960. In 1963, it was issued by Penguin Books as a Pelican, and remained in print for over twenty years. Since its disappearance, I have had a number of requests for it, and I am therefore particularly pleased that Ballantine has decided to reissue it.

The typescript was rejected by a number of publishers before Heinemann accepted it, including Cambridge University Press and Allen and Unwin. I still treasure a letter from the late Sir Stanley Unwin, dated 10th August, 1961.

Dear Sir,

An export [sic] who has been studying television programmes on our behalf to let us know what possibilities for books he observes arising from them, speaks most enthusiastically about you. . . .

We realise how busy you are, but if there is a possibility of your writing a book for us we should welcome the opportunity of publishing for you and would enter into an agreement right away.

Yours faithfully,
Stanley Unwin
Chairman

My reply was as follows.

Dear Sir Stanley Unwin,

    I am gratified by your invitation to write a book for you; but I am afraid I must decline it as I am already committed to Heinemann who have an option on my next two books.

    I find it a rather sad reflection on our times that the ephemeral medium of television should lead to such an invitation, whereas the offer of a manuscript produces only a rejection slip. In 1959 you were offered my book *The Integrity of the Personality* which you rejected. . . .

Since 1960, nine more books of mine have appeared, and I have also edited and annotated a collection of Jung's writings. It may therefore surprise some readers that, before I wrote *The Integrity of the Personality*, becoming an author had not occurred to me. I suppose that every author retains some special affection for his first published book. In my case, this is reinforced by the fact that I was forty years old when it appeared.

My reason for writing it was to clarify my own mind. Any appeal to a potential readership was entirely secondary. At the time, I had been qualified as a doctor for sixteen years, fourteen of which had been devoted to psychiatry. Although I had a wide experience of general psychiatry, and had been a consultant at various hospitals, my chief interest was in the practice of analytical psychotherapy. I had been trained in the school of Jung; but always remained aware that there were other schools and methods of psychotherapy which were equally effective.

I have never been an uncritical disciple or convert, and soon abandoned the label "Jungian." It seemed to me that the deplorable disputes between "Freudians," "Kleinians," "Jungians," and other varieties of psychotherapists were intensified by affirming allegiance to a particular group, as if this were a religious sect with a monopoly on "the truth."

Although I continued to owe a good deal to C. G. Jung's ideas, I could never accept them all. Moreover, I owed a debt to many other analytical writers, including unorthodox Freudians like John Bowlby and Ronald Fairbairn. This left me in the position of needing to define my own basic assumptions. As a practising psychotherapist, I could not dispense with some fundamental beliefs about human nature. But, since I was not able wholly to subscribe to any one set of beliefs advanced by any "guru," I had to fall back upon my own, however derivative. In trying to define my own assumptions, I hoped that I might attain greater objectivity; and, in the course of writing the book, also came to hope that I might make some small contribution to lessening the tensions between the various schools of psychotherapy. For, if people come to perceive that what they have in common is more important than any differences between them, it is possible that doctrinal dispute can be replaced by fruitful discussion. I still hold to the belief stated in the introduction; that the healing process in psychotherapy is directly related to the development of the relationship between the patient and the psychotherapist, and that the psychotherapist's attitude toward the patient is more important than the school to which he belongs.

The Integrity of the Personality was written over thirty years ago. Since then, I have changed—it would be awful if I had not done so. No doubt, if I were writing the book today, there would be changes of emphasis. For example, I have become more interested in the way individuals can deal with their own problems by making use of their creative potential in solitude, outside the bounds of any psychotherapeutic relationship. But, since I have written about this elsewhere, and since the book has been found useful in its present form, both by the "helping" professions and by their clients, I have decided to let it reappear without attempting to alter it.

Anthony Storr F.R.C.P., F.R.C.Psych., F.R.S.L.

INTRODUCTION

> *Philosophy alone can boast (and perhaps it is no more
> than the boast of philosophy), that her gentle hand is
> able to eradicate from the human mind the latent and
> deadly principle of fanaticism.*　　GIBBON[1]

Analytical psychotherapy is not, and probably never can
be, an exact science. The psychotherapeutic situation is
extremely intricate; a complex interaction between two im-
perfectly known variables—the therapist and the patient:
and, in spite of our efforts to make them so, our psychotherapeutic observations can never be entirely objective.
But it is not only the complexity of the relationship which
develops between patient and therapist which makes objectivity difficult: it is also the fact that the therapist cannot
avoid observing the patient from a particular point of view,
and is therefore bound to make certain assumptions about
him. The beliefs about human nature which the psychotherapist himself holds will partially determine both what
he finds in his patient, and also the relative emphasis which
he places upon his various findings. It is, therefore, important for the psychotherapist to be as aware as possible of
his own basic beliefs; for, although he may never attain
objectivity, he will certainly fall even further short of this
goal if he is unaware of the assumptions from which he is
proceeding.

This book is the attempt of a psychotherapist to define

in simple terms the basic hypotheses upon which his practice rests. Having become aware that one cannot practise psychotherapy without making certain assumptions about human nature, it seemed important to the author to try and find out what his own assumptions were. It may be that some people in an attempt to be scientific will deny that they have any fundamental beliefs, and will assert that what they have to say about psychopathology is the result of empirical observation only: but this assertion can always be shown to be false. It is impossible to make observations of any kind without an assumed framework. Let a historian support this contention. Herbert Butterfield[2] in *Christianity and History* says:

> It is a mistake for writers of history and other teachers to imagine that if they are not Christian they are refraining from committing themselves, or working without any doctrine at all, discussing History without any presuppositions. Amongst historians, as in other fields, the blindest of all the blind are those who are unable to examine their own presuppositions, and blithely imagine therefore that they do not possess any.

If this is true for the historian it is certainly true for the psychotherapist: and it seems vital that the latter should try to be aware of what frame of reference he is using; for it is only if he is aware of it that he will be able to alter it if the facts demand that he should do so. An immense edifice of thought like psychoanalysis or analytical psychology can easily become a closed circle of ideas in which every observation is referred to an existing hypothesis without ever questioning the hypothesis itself: and the structure can become so complex that it is extremely difficult to disinter the basic hypotheses upon which it rests.

There is a widespread idea that the man of science holds no theories in his own field except upon evidence. This is not so. Scientists, like novelists or poets, have their own vision of the universe; and their vision is not based primarily upon evidence. Einstein,[3] for instance, says: "A theory can be proved by experiment; but no path leads from experiment to the birth of a theory." But, although a scientific theory is not based primarily on evidence, no scientist will rest content with a theory which remains unsupported; and he will be ready to alter his theory if he can find no evidence to sustain it. In this he differs from the artist, whose vision is its own justification and who does not need to relate his vision so closely to the brute facts of the external world—and so has no reason to alter it provided it continues to please him.

In their efforts to be scientific and to restrict what they have to say about human nature only to such facts as can be proved by experiment, the academic psychologists have been forced to omit so much of what is obviously important about human beings that to many people their findings appear sterile. But even the experiments of the most laboratory-minded psychologist rest upon unproved hypotheses, and are bound to do so: and whereas the laboratory worker is free to restrict himself to limited aspects of human nature, the psychotherapist must deal with the whole man, and may have to work with hypotheses which are not only unproved but probably unprovable.

Even the measurement of intelligence rests upon the hypothesis that there is a more or less discrete function of the mind which we can designate as "the intelligence"; a hypothesis which is not easy to substantiate: and it is with pleasure that the psychotherapist finds a research worker in a psychology laboratory recognizing this. A. W. Heim[4] in her book *The Appraisal of Intelligence* says:

> A review of the material collected by testers of intelligence suggests a number of underlying presuppositions, some of which I should like to criticize. These presuppositions have sometimes been publicly discussed and discredited, yet most of the work on intelligence testing continues implicitly to assume their truth. First is the evident belief that there exists some one attribute "intelligence," which is one-dimensional, measurable, capable of quantitative but not qualitative differences and, therefore, capable of strictly quantitative comparison.

This is the attitude of mind which, I believe, the psychotherapist should cultivate; although it is even more difficult for him to do so than it is for workers in fields less directly concerned with human passions. Because of the very nature of his subject, the psychotherapist is bound to work with concepts which are of emotional, as well as intellectual, significance. The Oedipus complex makes more affective impact than Boyle's law; and we are predisposed to feel more strongly about the former than about the latter. The strength of supposition is a subject of great psychological interest, and it may be tentatively suggested that a hierarchy could be established in which hypothesis would represent one end of a scale and delusion the other, with the term belief somewhere in between. A hypothesis is, by definition, provisional; a notion which can be modified at any time by the discovery of new facts which do not support it. A belief is more emotionally toned, and requires a change, not only of thought, but of heart, to alter it. A delusion cannot be modified—for the whole personality is attacked if the delusion is undermined—and, whatever facts may be adduced against it, it remains unshaken. It is the emotional strength with which a delusion is held that is its chief characteristic—not its falsity. Every one of us has false beliefs; but these do not amount to delusions because they can be modified if necessity demands it. But delusions may be the only things which render life tolerable, and, as such, are jealously defended against all the assaults of reason.

Psychotherapy is by its very nature concerned with the basic themes of human life. Love and hate, birth and death, sexuality and power: all the vast complexities of the emotions which stir and sway the hearts of men are the daily concern of the psychotherapist. Even if he wishes to, it would be impossible for him to avoid having some views as to the meaning and significance of the momentous themes with which he is concerned, some theoretical framework to which he could relate the inchoate mass of human problems with which he is presented. The psychotherapist's views are bound, because of his subject matter, to be more in the nature of beliefs than of hypotheses; and we may be content if they are not so emotionally held as to amount to delusions.

Whitehead[5] in *Science and the Modern World* wrote: "Every philosophy is tinged with the colouring of some secret imaginative background which never emerges explicitly into its train of reasoning." So is every psychology; and it may be that some of the difficulties in communication between the various analytical schools could be resolved if more analysts were prepared to state, with clarity and simplicity, the beliefs about human nature which constitute the inevitable background to their work. At present, it is rather as if each group were using different geometries without being aware that they were doing so. It is well known that any number of geometries can be invented. Euclid's is not the only one; equally valid and internally consistent geometries exist which rest upon different basic assumptions and have their own special fields of applicability. Euclid, however, stated his basic assumptions quite clearly: and so, no doubt, did Riemann, Minkowski, and the rest. Let us try to do the same in psychopathology. We need not mind if our basic assumptions are unproven: so are the basic assumptions of any science.

The physical sciences from the seventeenth century to the beginning of the twentieth century rested upon the basic hypothesis that Nature conformed to a causal, deterministic scheme: and it was reasonable to assume that, if a man was an experimental scientist, he shared a common substratum of belief with other experimental scientists about the nature of the universe and the laws which governed it. In this scheme the physical world was thought to be both external to the scientist and unaffected by his observation of it. It was assumed that the universe was governed by a set of immutable rules—the Laws of Nature. The behaviour of every particle of matter was thought to be determined by preceding events, and the future supposed to be governed absolutely by the past. All that was needed for the whole truth to be discovered was that a series of brilliant observers should disinter more and more of the facts until the whole natural order lay exposed before man's eyes as the workings of a complicated clock might lie exposed to the gaze of a watchmaker.

The influence of this conventional, and now outmoded, scientific point of view has long been so enormous that, even though scientists can no longer subscribe to it, anyone who attempts to make observations which could conceivably be called scientific is bound to be influenced by it; and to tend to regard the observations which he makes as being independent both of himself and of his particular view of the world. The physicists abandoned this "objective" view when they found that, if a particle was both small and fast-moving, they could not determine both its position and its velocity; for they were unable to observe it without altering its behaviour. Heisenberg's Uncertainty Principle defined a limit beyond which prediction could not go; and it became generally realized that the observer and what was observed could not be separated.

In the complex task of trying to observe another human being, all except the least sophisticated of psychotherapists will have realized that the object of their inquiry is altered by their observations. The very fact of being in the same room with another human creature, as opposed to being alone, affects behaviour, and the complexity of the relationship between therapist and patient is such that anyone might justifiably doubt whether objective observation of the patient is possible on these grounds alone. The view that the psychotherapist is a wholly detached observer and the patient a piece of mechanism which is unaffected by his scrutiny cannot be sustained: and although a fair degree of objectivity may ultimately be reached, I believe this to be an achievement on the part of both therapist and patient, rather than a condition which ever obtains in the initial stages of the therapeutic relationship, or, indeed, in the initial stages of any other human relationship.

Physicists, however, are in no better case. Heisenberg[6] himself says:

Science no longer confronts nature as an objective observer, but sees itself as an actor in the interplay between man and nature. The scientific method of analysing, explaining, and classifying has become conscious of its limitations, which arise out of the fact that by its intervention science alters and refashions the object of investigation. In other words, method and object can no longer be separated. The scientific world-view has ceased to be a scientific view in the true sense of the word.

The interactions between observer and observed is one reason why it is difficult to assess the psychotherapeutic situation in terms of the conventional viewpoint of science: it is not the only one. In the scheme formerly put forward by science there is no place for free-will. For, if the behaviour of every particle of matter is determined by preceding events, and the future governed absolutely by the past, the idea of free-will is inadmissible.

But the psychotherapist cannot, I believe, exclude free-will from his scheme of things. Even if he assumes that the majority of psychological events are strictly determined, he is still bound to behave as though both he and his patient had some faculty of selection, some potentiality of choosing between alternative courses of action, some power, however limited, of determining their own future. Although such a concept has no place in the older scientific view, modern physics has no objection to it; and as long ago as 1928 Eddington[7] stated in his Gifford lectures:

The future is a combination of the causal influences of the past together with unpredictable elements—unpredictable not merely because it is impracticable to obtain the data of prediction, but because no data connected causally with our experience exist. It will be necessary to defend so remarkable a change of opinion at some length. Meanwhile we may note that science thereby withdraws its moral opposition to free-will. Those who maintain a deterministic theory of mental activity must do so as the outcome of their study of the mind itself and not with the idea that they are thereby making it more comfortable with our experimental knowledge of the laws of inorganic nature.

The philosophical position of science is no longer the same as it was sixty years ago. Science has shifted its ground, and is beginning to be more interested in the subjective determinants of the patterns which scientists project upon the world. This is not to deny the existence of an objective order of the universe; but rather a realization that the observer as well as the observed has to be included in the scheme of things, and that to exclude him is to be unscientific.

Professor W. Pauli[8] for example says:

In contrast to the purely empirical conception according to which natural laws can with virtual certainty be derived from the material of experience alone, many physicists have recently emphasized anew the fact that intuition and the direction of attention play a considerable role in the development of the concepts and idea, generally far transcending mere experience, that are necessary for the erection of a system of natural laws (that is, a scientific theory).

It seems, therefore, both reasonable and desirable that psychotherapists should be prepared to make subjective statements about the concepts with which they work. Paradoxically enough, it is through such subjectivity that a greater objectivity may ultimately come, as I have tried to explain above. In the process of trying to delineate my own assumptions, I found that certain ideas about the nature of the psychotherapeutic process developed which seemed to provide a tentative explanation of it in rather simple and more general terms than those usually employed by analysts.

T. H. Huxley[9] once wrote:

> All science starts with hypotheses—in other words, with assumptions that are unproved, while they may be, and often are, erroneous, but which are better than nothing to the searcher after order in the maze of phenomena. And the historical process of every science depends on the criticism of hypotheses—on the gradual stripping off, that is, of their untrue or superfluous parts—until there remains only that exact verbal expression of as much as we know of the facts, and no more, which constitutes a perfect scientific theory.

We are very far indeed from having a perfect scientific theory of psychotherapy; but, if we are prepared to examine our hypotheses we may be able to strip them of a few of their superfluous parts. I have been trained both as a general psychiatrist and as an analyst in the school of Jung; and I therefore approach psychotherapy in terms of this training. But I am not so doctrinaire as to imagine that my own particular point of view is the only possible one. I am aware that, for instance, my Freudian and Kleinian colleagues obtain results with patients which are neither worse nor better than my own; and, although there are probably some patients temperamentally better served by being treated in terms of a particular discipline, it is difficult to defend the idea that any one analytical school surpasses any other in the results achieved.

It has long seemed to me probable that the analytical attitude to the patient is far more important than the school to which the analyst belongs; and that, in selecting a psychotherapist, it is more valuable to know whether he is capable of the right attitude to the patient than to know which theory of personality he holds. For, if the results obtained by different analytical approaches are comparable, it cannot be that the patient improves by discovering the truth about himself—there are too many "truths" for this to be credible.

Every psychotherapeutic situation, however, contains a therapist and a patient; and it seems likely that the healing process is directly related to the development of the relationship between them. It is hoped that this book may be taken not only as a subjective statement, but also as some contribution towards understanding this therapeutic relationship.

CHAPTER 1

SELF-REALIZATION

The most conspicuous mark of the moral level of any community is the value it sets on human personality.

STREETER[1]

Psychotherapists of different persuasions appear to share at least one basic hypothesis: the notion that the individual human being is of value, and that it is important that each individual should be able to develop his own personality in as unrestricted and complete a way as possible.

Any practising psychotherapist who reflects upon his daily activity can hardly fail to be aware that, explicitly or implicitly, he is attributing to the individual a very high value indeed. Psychotherapy which involves more than superficial guidance is bound to be of some length, often of very considerable length: and there can be few psychotherapists who have not asked themselves whether or not it is worth while spending weeks, months, and years giving time and consideration to the problems of the small number of persons whom he has time to treat. Should he not rather be employing his abilities in wider fields and devoting himself to problems which transcend the merely individual? Most psychotherapists would, I believe, reply to this that the individual was to them more important than any impersonal problem, and that to help even one individual to reach a solution of his difficulties was an achievement not only satisfactory in itself but one which might be far-reaching in its effects; for, as is generally known, neurosis affects not only the sufferer, but all those who are emotionally involved with him. The analytical investigation of the human mind is in itself a fascinating task; but, unless there was a strong propensity to value individual personalities highly, it is hard to believe that so many psychotherapists would devote so much time to helping so few people, however much they might justify their efforts by reference to the wide results of treating a single case. It is true, of course, that it is by the practice of psychotherapy that the psychotherapist makes his living: but, even within the limited field of psychiatry, there are other and more profitable ways of earning a livelihood, any of which will make less demand upon the psychiatrist, although some may give him more administrative power.

This belief in the importance and value of the individual personality which seems to underlie the clinical endeavours of psychotherapists of every school is widely held as part of the liberal humanist tradition, and perhaps most educated people in Great Britain and the U.S.A. would subscribe to it. We are fortunate to have been reared in a country and in an age where such a belief can flourish, and where, slowly but surely, the importance of the individual is being increasingly realized in different spheres of activity. In medicine, for instance, the view that it is the individual as well as the disease which needs treatment is gradually gaining ground, and many physicians would now agree that to separate the two was unscientific. It used to be sufficient in treating peptic ulcer, for instance, to put the patient to bed, prescribe a suitable diet and alkalis and, when his ulcer had healed, as it usually did, dismiss him with the satisfaction that correct medical treatment had had the happy result of curing the disorder. Moreover, no hint of criticism of the patient entered into the attitude of the physician, who regarded him as an unfortunate sufferer attacked by an unpleasant disease; and who, although he might recognize an "ulcer-type" who tended to drive himself harder than other men, thought it no part of his duty to investigate more deeply the patient's personality and fundamental attitudes to life. And yet, however incomplete and speculative psychosomatic medicine may be, it is increasingly obvious that many important diseases cannot be treated as if they were enemies from without attacking an unfortunate man. Many illnesses are more in the nature of assaults from within: they are inseparable from the man himself, from his personality, his attitude to life, and, consequently, the way he lives his life. Men who are continually anxious, or who, in the pursuit of success, drive themselves too hard, or who through fear of superior authority strive desperately to be perfect in all that they do, are more likely to develop the common chronic psychosomatic disorders; and any treatment which omits all consideration of the personality is bound to be incomplete.

Were Samuel Butler to return to earth he might well be amused at the turn of events in the democracies, which appear to be emulating the Erewhonians. It will be recalled that in Erewhon disease was punished with the severest penalties, whereas criminal conduct occasioned only commiseration and concern. We are not yet so advanced as the Erewhonians, but it is nevertheless true that we attribute less deliberate malice to the criminal, and hold the invalid to be more responsible for his illness, than at any other period in our civilization.

The changing criminal law also reflects the increasing awareness of the importance of personality. It is the criminal as a person who has to be dealt with; it is insufficient to punish the crime without reference to the person who committed it. Although the Law is, and must continue to be, no respecter of persons in its definitions of what is, and what is not, legal: yet, in dealing with the transgressor, it is of the utmost importance that the Law should pay more attention to the person than to the crime which he has committed. A boy of sixteen who has stolen needs very different treatment from a recidivist of fifty who has committed the same offence, and recent legislation is happily taking this more and more into account.

The increasing importance which is attributed to the individual is confined to those countries in which the régime is more or less a liberal one, and is notably absent from the totalitarian states. Where the State is exalted to the supreme value, the individual is no longer important in his own right, but only in so far as he serves the State. The vision of serving a common purpose, of losing one's individuality in the pursuit of an ideal, is an attractive one for many people; but it is generally true that when men become possessed by a vision they abandon humanity and tend to treat their fellows abominably. History is full of instances of individuals being sacrificed to ideas, and human values subordinated to abstractions. The conviction that there was but one path to salvation and that any departure from this path was dangerous heresy made it possible for the officials of the Inquisition to justify, at any rate to themselves, the most revolting treatment of those who disagreed with them: for they argued that, as no torment upon earth could possibly equal the perpetual pains of damnation, any torture could legitimately be employed to force heretics into submission to the authority of the Church, and thus save their souls, even at the expense of destroying their bodies.

The vision of the brotherhood of man which is at the root of the Communist ideology has seduced many able minds into tolerating present inhumanities for the sake of future liberty, equality, and fraternity. The pursuit of the millennium, as Professor Cohn has recently demonstrated, is not only a mythical, but also a destructive, quest in which men become ready to sacrifice not only their own lives but those of others to an illusion, and to annihilate their fellows in the name of brotherly love.

It is not surprising that the two most original and creative figures in modern psychiatry, Freud and Jung, were both proscribed by the Nazis, although only Freud was Jewish: for both, though holding widely divergent views, upheld the value of the individual personality, and could never therefore acknowledge the supremacy of the State.

It is clear that psychotherapists concur in valuing the individual personality highly, and, however much they might differ about the process of development, they would also agree that personality was an achievement, not simply a datum of genetics. To be oneself, to realize one's own personality to its fullest extent, is to develop from childhood to maturity; and every psychotherapeutic system is concerned with this development. I have suggested that the results of psychotherapy in different hands do not vary so widely as the hypotheses upon which the different forms of psychotherapy rest. This can, I think, be elaborated by stating that the end-result which is aimed at (but never, perhaps, achieved) is the same in every system: which is probably why the results of different approaches are comparable. Whether the supposition is that all neurotic symptoms are connected with unresolved infantile sexuality, or whether it is assumed that they are due to an unslaked appetite for power; to a failure to reach maturity in social relationships, or to a lack of harmony between the rational and irrational functions of the mind; yet the picture of the man who is free, who has reached maturity, is implicitly the same, whether he be called integrated, individuated, or whole. In one system the touchstone of maturity is the ability to have satisfactory genital relationships with the opposite sex; in another to be in harmony with society; in another to be free of libidinal ties to introjected bad objects; in another to be individuated: but all these pictures are, I believe, ways of expressing the same essential condition. It is the way of achieving the end, the means, and the details which are in dispute, not the final achievement.

I propose to call this final achievement self-realization, by which I mean the fullest possible expression in life of the innate potentialities of the individual, the realization of his own uniqueness as a personality: and I also put forward the hypothesis that, consciously or unconsciously, every man is seeking this goal. This might serve as a working hypothesis to which psychotherapists of varying persuasions could subscribe; and many would go further and say that the purpose of psychotherapy was not simply to relieve symptoms but to enable the patient to realize himself more fully than he had previously been able to do.

The use of the word "goal" will certainly excite critical comment from those who decry psychology as being unscientific, since such a concept has no place in the mechanical, deterministic universe which was the ideal of nineteenth-century physics. In describing the motions of the planets one need not ask what goal they are seeking; but in describing human behaviour it is, I believe, necessary to ask this question, and unscientific to omit it. Many processes in nature are only fully comprehensible in terms of the end-result or goal, and remain obscure if considered simply from the causal point of view. The concept of "goal-seeking" is, for instance, of central importance in cybernetics.

W. R. Ashby,[2] writing on "The Cerebral Mechanisms of Intelligent Action," says:

> Physiologists accept the working hypothesis that the brain acts as a machine. They have succeeded in elucidating the nature of the mechanisms responsible for many of the simpler and more primitive reactions, but to discover the nature of the mechanisms responsible for other "higher" processes has been more difficult: the material is more intricate and the concepts are more subtle.
>
> Among these "higher" processes a property fundamental from the biological point of view is the ability of the organism to be "goal-seeking," to seek with persistence a few basic goals through an almost infinite variety of circumstances, and by a great variety of means.

It is clear that it is as legitimate to ask towards what end a process is directed, as to inquire from what cause it originated, and I believe that any psychological description of human beings must attempt to answer both questions. The highly complicated facts of human behaviour can be related to both inquiries; and whilst some facts are better explained in terms of what has happened in the individual's past, others are more easily comprehended in terms of the goal toward which the individual appears to be striving. Neither description is complete without the other.

A child, for instance, behaves aggressively towards its mother. From one point of view this behaviour may be explained in terms of the restrictive, over-anxious attitude of the mother, who will not allow the child sufficient liberty. From the other, the aggressiveness is an assertion of independence on the part of the child, an attempt to act as a separate individual in its own right, and therefore an important step on the road to maturity. Parents are commonly blamed for the aggressive behaviour of their children, and in many instances censure is justified; but, if the children are to become independent, they are bound to rebel, however enlightened the parental discipline may be, and so parents sometimes find themselves criticized where their only fault is that they are parents. Parents are "good" in so far as they are protective, and "bad" in so far as they are restrictive: and since protection is impossible without restriction no parent can escape this double appellation. This, however, is in parenthesis; but the point is made that the description of the child's behaviour is incomplete unless both the forces acting on it from without and those impelling it from within are taken into account.

If we postulate an innate drive towards self-realization, an instinctive force impelling the individual towards an ever more complete expression of his latent potentialities, we shall be able to understand much which might otherwise remain obscure in psychology. In biology, it has been found necessary to postulate "organizers," which, in the immature organism, regulate the processes of growth and development. Our psychological concept of an inner urge towards self-realization is not dissimilar.

It may be advisable to point out, at this early stage in my argument, that self-realization does not imply any lack of recognition of individual differences. Men vary in innumerable ways; in intelligence, physique, temperament, and so on. It is by no means implied that men should strive after any goal which is beyond their individual capacities. What is implied is that, whatever their basic endowments, the possibility of reaching a certain harmony, an inner wholeness, and a satisfactory relationship between themselves and the world is innate in all men; and that this is as true of the less highly as of the more highly gifted.

It is the psychotherapist's task to help his patients to be more themselves, to realize themselves more fully. Whatever method he employs, whatever school he adheres to, and through whatever spectacles he views the universe, his basic aim is to help his patient to live his own life more completely, without trying to order that life for him or to convert the patient to his own frame of reference.

CHAPTER 2

THE RELATIVITY OF PERSONALITY

Imagine yourself alone in the midst of nothingness, and then try to tell me how large you are. EDDINGTON[1]

If self-realization is accepted as a basic hypothesis, it should be possible to counter the first and most obvious criticism which will be brought to bear upon it. The interests of the individual, it may be argued, may clash with the society in which he lives. A society of individualists each pursuing his own ends regardless of the needs of others is an impossibility. Self-realization cannot be the end of man, for it is inconsistent with his social existence.

This is the point of view put forward by Bertrand Russell[2] in his *History of Western Philosophy*: "Man is not a solitary animal, and so long as social life survives, self-realization cannot be the supreme principle of ethics."

This statement is of great interest on account of its implications. I think every psychotherapist would agree that man is not a solitary animal. So much psychotherapeutic work is concerned with the exploration of inter-personal relationships that the psychotherapist is unlikely to disregard the need of men for each other. But if man is not a solitary animal, his efforts to realize his own personality, his attempts at individuation, must include relationships with others. Russell is implying that it is only at the expense of other people that a man can be himself, and illustrates his thesis by the example of Byron, whose egotism was notorious. But Byronic self-seeking, which Russell rightly condemns, is, as the psychotherapist sees it, immature, childish behaviour which is very far from self-realization just because it results in the alienation of others and consequently in isolation. If men could develop their own personalities only by disregarding the needs of others, self-realization would indeed be a hopeless and evil principle. A society of ruthless *entrepreneurs* is bound to be anarchic and ultimately self-destructive; and this seems to be the sort of society which Russell anticipates as the result of encouraging the development of the individual. In communities which are so poor that the majority of individuals are living below the subsistence level, it is probably true that a man could only begin to develop his potentialities at the expense of his fellows. The demands of an empty belly take precedence over psychological maturity, and freedom from want is a necessary precursor to the refinements of emotional development. In civilizations like our own, however, where the whole of a man's energy is not necessarily committed to keeping himself and his family alive, the development of the individual proceeds not at the expense, but rather to the advantage, of those people with whom he has to do. It is the child who has to prove himself better than others; and a compulsive striving for power is one characteristic of emotional immaturity. The adult, however, if he has obtained a position in which such talents as he has can be of use, will discover that his fellows are not obstacles, but rather aids, in the expression of his potentialities.

I believe that the development of the individual and the maturity of his personal relationships proceed hand-in-hand, and that one cannot take place without the other.

Self-realization is not an anti-social principle; it is firmly based on the fact that men need each other in order to be themselves, and that those people who succeed in achieving the greatest degree of independence and maturity are also those who have the most satisfactory relationships with others. Psychiatrists of every school have, for many years, laid stress on the child's need for independence; and it is generally agreed that much neurotic suffering is due to failure to become sufficiently independent of the early environment. But we have grown so used to thinking of independence as a desirable goal that we may easily misconstrue it. Independence is not the same as isolation, and no human being is, in my view, self-sufficient. If such a creature as a self-sufficient human being existed, he would no longer possess those characteristics which we call human, and indeed could scarcely be said to exist as a personality.

> No man is an Iland, intire of it selfe; every man
> is a peece of the Continent, a part of the Maine; if
> a Clod bee washed away by the Sea, Europe is the
> lesse, as well as if a Mannor of they friends or of
> theire owne were; any man's death diminishes me,
> because I am involved in Mankinde; And therefore
> never send to know for whom the bell tolls; it tolls
> for thee.

In incomparable language Donne[3] affirms his belief in the fundamental bond between one man and another; the link which attests our sharing of the human condition. We are all, inescapably, members one of another; and no one can achieve independence and maturity in isolation from his fellows. It is in recognition of this that Fairbairn, whose reformulation of Freudian psychopathology will, I believe, gain increasing acceptance, designates the final stage of emotional development "Mature Dependence." By this juxtaposition of two words which, at first sight, might seem ill-assorted, he is affirming his belief that a man is incomplete without satisfying personal relationships; and is indicating his recognition of the fact that the full development of personality implies an acceptance of the basic need of men for each other.

Personality is, of course, a relative concept. We can enumerate the various traits of personality which a man exhibits. We can say that he is decided, or gentle, or rapacious; that he is unfeeling, or stupid, or judicious; but our epithets have no meaning in isolation, just as black has no meaning without white. If by personality we mean a man's "distinctive personal character" we are obliged to recognize that we can only conceive of such an entity in terms of contrasting it with other distinctive personal characters. The epithets which we apply to people are easily seen to be meaningless except as relative terms: I believe the same to be true of the total entity of the personality.

The more isolated a man is, the less is he an independent personality, and the less does he exhibit those qualities which distinguish one man from another. When it is impossible to make a relationship with someone, we tend to call him psychotic, and psychiatrists often base their diagnosis of schizophrenia, in part, on their subjective inability to make any contact with the patient. Schizophrenics are probably the most isolated people in the world. They are also quite remarkably alike. One of the most striking features of the chronic wards of any mental hospital (and the chronic wards contain a high proportion of schizophrenics) is the lack of contact between the patients. Men may sleep in the next bed to each other, and eat at table together for thirty years and never exchange a word; each locked in his private world, each so apparently self-sufficient that he has to be cared for all his life. And it is remarkable how, *pari passu* with his isolation, the schizophrenic suffers a loss of personal identity. The repetitive sameness of paranoid delusions, the stereotypy of schizophrenic thought, may surprise the untrained observer and be too little regarded by the psychiatrist. Different patients say exactly the same thing in almost identical words: that their mother is poisoning them, that they are being influenced by electricity, that their bodies are being destroyed. They are clearly reporting the same experience, and so it is natural that their way of expressing it should be similar; but the loss of personal identity goes far beyond this, as will be recognized by anyone who has worked in a mental hospital. In the absence of relationship with others, men become more alike, not more individual; and isolation leads ultimately to a loss of the distinguishing features of personality not, as might be supposed, to their intensification. Conrad[4] knew this, as is shown by his description of the suicide of Martin Decoud in *Nostromo*. Decoud is left alone on a small uninhabited island. On the tenth day of his solitude he rows out to sea and shoots himself.

> But the truth was that he died from solitude, the enemy known to but few on this earth, and whom only the simplest of us are fit to withstand. The brilliant Costaguanero of the boulevards had died from solitude and want of faith in himself and others. . . . The brilliant "Son Decoud," the spoilt darling of the family, the lover of Antonia and journalist of Sulaco, was not fit to grapple with himself

single-handed. Solitude from mere outward condition of existence becomes very swiftly a state of soul in which the affectations of irony and scepticism have no place. It takes possession of the mind, and drives forth the thought into the exile of utter unbelief. After three days of waiting for the sight of some human face, Decoud caught himself entertaining a doubt of his own individuality. It had merged into the world of cloud and water, of natural forces and forms of nature. In our activity alone do we find the sustaining illusion of an independent existence as against the whole scheme of things of which we form a helpless part.

It has frequently been observed that even the most deteriorated schizophrenic improves to some extent if a nurse, an occupational therapist, or a doctor takes a sustained personal interest in him. Whatever the ultimate "cause" of schizophrenia, or whatever one's views as to its psychopathology, there can be no doubt that the development of a relationship between the schizophrenic and another person leads to improvement in his mental condition. This is affirmed in a recent paper by Thomas Freeman and Andrew McGhie[5] on "The Psychopathology of Schizophrenia."

One final word. Our scepticism of psychopathological theory in schizophrenia does not imply a nihilistic attitude towards the psychological treatment of schizophrenia. We have no doubt that all schizophrenic patients can be improved by the development of a preverbal, effective relationship between patient and doctor or nurse. The extent to which this relationship develops and deepens determines how far the patient will return along the road to mental health.

Erich Fromm[6] in *The Fear of Freedom* says: "To feel completely alone and isolated leads to mental disintegration just as physical starvation leads to death." One might add that to be completely related to another person is to be most oneself, to affirm one's personality in its totality.

And so we have the paradox that man is at his most individual when most in contact with his fellows, and is least of all a separate individual when detached from them.

What is it that is so important about relationship with others that a man cannot develop his own personality without it? I believe that, just as a child cannot do without the affection and love of its parents, so the adult cannot dispense with the acceptance of his fellow men—or if he does so, is faced with the isolation of insanity. To know that another person accepts one just as one is, unconditionally, is to be able to accept oneself, and therefore to be able to *be* oneself, to realize one's own personality. One cannot even begin to be conscious of oneself as a separate individual without another person with whom to compare oneself. A man in isolation is a collective man, a man without individuality. People often express the idea that they are most themselves when they are alone; and creative artists especially may believe that it is in the ivory towers of the solitary expression of their art that their innermost being finds its completion. They forget that art is communication, and that, implicitly or explicitly, the work which they produce in solitude is aimed at somebody. Virginia Woolf[7] in *The Common Reader* once wrote an essay on this theme called "The Patron and the Crocus."

Thus the writer who has been moved by the sight of the first crocus in Kensington Gardens has, before he sets pen to paper, to choose from a crowd of competitors the particular patron who suits him best. It is futile to say, "Dismiss them all; think only of your crocus," because writing is a method of communication; and the crocus is an imperfect crocus until it has been shared. The first man or the last may write for himself alone, but he is an exception and an unenviable one at that, and the gulls are welcome to his works if the gulls can read them.

Painting produced by psychotic patients, whether for therapeutic reasons or not, may be interesting but is seldom aesthetically moving, partly because the attempt to communicate is lacking; and studies of the paintings of artists who have become psychotic show a deterioration in the quality of their products after the onset of their illness.

There is an interesting study of "doodles" which may serve to underline this point. The authors[8] took advantage of a newspaper competition to collect and classify 9,000 examples of this kind of drawing. In their words doodles are "graphic results of playful activity done without purpose, in a state of divided and/or diminished attention." Doodles are, therefore, a good example of a graphic production which is completely autistic; that is, *not* designed for communication. As the authors say:

Doodling can be called a most asocial activity. . . . Each individual example taken from this material was made in an atmosphere of complete isolation of the individual, for which imprisonment in a telephone box can be taken as the standard

symbol. . . . The isolation, freedom, and independence from standard influences, had not the effect
one might have expected. The products of free fantasy were conformable with a few types, and to a
large extent could be called monotonous. . . . It is
interesting to see that in spite of the segregation
and isolation of the doodler, trends of collective
psychology become active.

We may be grateful for the observations of our authors
while not sharing their surprise. According to the hypothesis propounded above it is exactly under conditions of segregation that one would expect trends of collective, as
opposed to individual, psychology to become active. Here
again is evidence that lack of communication leads to uniformity and stereotypy; whereas the true work of art is an
expression of an effort towards relationship, a desire on the
part of the artist to communicate—not an autistic fantasy.

The observation that men become less and not more
individual when alone does not imply that solitude has no
value in the development of personality. Indeed, periods of
solitude may be effective in promoting an interest in, and
encouraging a return to, those problems of existence which
are common to all men. Such reports as we have seem to
support the idea that, when men are solitary for any length
of time, they inevitably become preoccupied with ultimate
questions; those questions of good and evil, of meaning and
purpose, and of man's place in the universe, which have
engaged the interest of speculative minds throughout the
centuries. It is the habit of those who found religions to
retreat from the world for a time, and both Christ and Mo-
hammed found it necessary to retire into the desert before
proclaiming their respective revelations. Such expeditions

may be *reculer pour mieux sauter*, a valuable renewal of contact with fundamentals; but it is necessary to return to contact with humanity if the retreat is to enrich the development of the individual and those with whom he is linked. The desert may evoke a concern with ultimates, but it is no substitute for relationships in the maturing of personality.

CHAPTER 3

THE MATURE RELATIONSHIP

Through the Thou a man becomes I.   BUBER[1]

In the last chapter it was suggested that a man can neither develop nor realize his personality in isolation; and that maturity of the individual personality and maturity in relationships with other people go hand in hand. But what is maturity? Can we describe or reach agreement upon what is a mature relationship? This is by no means an easy question to answer, since the concept of a mature relationship depends upon subjective assumptions which are deeply rooted. It is interesting to note that, in the index to *The Psychoanalytic Theory of Neurosis*, Fenichel's masterly compendium, the word maturity does not occur; and while it is easy to discover what various writers think is immature, it is more difficult to find what idea they have of maturity.

The psycho-analytic concept of maturity derived from the work of Abraham used to be comprised by the phrase "genital primacy"; and, for some psychoanalysts, the ability to have satisfying genital relationships with the opposite sex constitutes the acid test of maturity in interpersonal relationships. It is true that certain psycholanalysts are dissatisfied with this test. Marjorie Brierley,[2] for instance, in her *Trends in Psycho-Analysis* says:

But experience testifies that . . . genital potency with incapacity for personal appreciation of the sexual partner, is by no means uncommon; it is, perhaps, more frequent among men, where its development may have been aided by the long tradition of "feminine inferiority."

The term "personal appreciation" is not defined or enlarged upon; and this is, to my mind, a regrettable omission; for it is this "personal appreciation" which I believe to be the final expression of maturity in human relationships. In a famous passage Jung[3] describes what he conceives to be the ideal relationship between doctor and patient in the therapeutic situation.

If the doctor wants to offer guidance to another, or even to accompany him a step of the way, he must be in touch with this other person's psychic life. He is never in touch when he passes judgement. Whether he puts his judgement into words, or keeps them to himself, makes not the slightest difference. To take the opposite position, and to agree with the patient offhand, is also of no use, but estranges him as much as condemnation. We can get in touch with another person only by an attitude of unprejudiced objectivity. This may sound like a scientific precept, and may be confused with a purely intellectual and detached attitude of mind. But what I mean to convey is something quite different. It is a human quality—a kind of deep respect for facts and events and for the person who suffers from them—a respect for the secret of such a human life.

It may be objected that this statement refers to a special situation, that between doctor and patient; but, as Jung constantly emphasizes, the doctor is himself always involved in the therapeutic situation as a person; and I do not think that it misrepresents Jung's views to quote this passage as an example of his picture of what a human relationship should be. In this extract, it will be noted that the ideal of "unprejudiced objectivity" occupies a middle position between two opposites which are expressed as "passing judgement" on the one hand, and "agreeing offhand" on the other. To be in touch with another person, therefore, is to recognize his difference from oneself, and, at the same time, to respect this difference. To pass judgement is to imply that the other person should alter himself; to agree offhand is to imply that one's own attitude is less valid than that of the other person. The ideal is a relationship in which each respects the other as a person in his own right, without trying to alter the other.

In the last chapter mention was made of the concept of "Mature Dependence" which is the name that Fairbairn[4] gives to his final stage of emotional development. Here is what he says about it:

What distinguishes mature dependence from infantile dependence is that it is characterized neither by a one-sided attitude of incorporation nor by an attitude of primary emotional identification. On the contrary, it is characterized by a capacity on the part of a differentiated individual for cooperative relationships with differentiated objects. So far as the appropriate biological object is concerned, the relationship is, of course, genital; but it is a relationship involving evenly matched giving and taking between two differentiated individuals who are mutually dependent, and between whom there is no disparity of dependence. Further, the relationship is characterized by an absence of primary identification and an absence of incorporation. At least, this is the ideal picture; but it is, of course, never completely realized in practice, since there is no one whose libidinal development proceeds wholly without a hitch.

This is a much more elaborate statement than Jung's—but I believe the underlying idea to be the same. It is interesting that both writers start with negatives: the ideal is neither X nor Y, but something which is either between the two, or which transcends both. Scylla is, for Jung, passing judgement; for Fairbairn, one-sided incorporation. Charybdis is, for Fairbairn, primary emotional identification; for Jung, offhand agreement.

The attitudes described by Fairbairn as incorporation and identification are connected with, and may underlie, the more familiar concepts of dominance and submission, or sadism and masochism. To incorporate another person is to swallow him up, to overwhelm him, and to destroy him; and thus to treat him ultimately as less than a whole person. To identify with another person is to lose oneself, to submerge one's own identity in that of the other, to be overwhelmed, and hence to treat oneself ultimately as less than a whole person. To pass judgement, in Jung's sense, is to place oneself in an attitude of superiority; to agree offhandedly is to place oneself in an attitude of inferiority. Scylla and Charybdis are graphic representations of psychological truths: the personality can cease to exist in two ways—either by destroying the other, or by being absorbed by the other—and maturity in interpersonal relationships demands that neither oneself nor the other shall disappear, but that each shall contribute to the affirmation and realization of the other's personality.

Although both attitudes are equally destructive of mature relationships, we tend, in our pseudo-Christian democracy, to condemn the one more than the other. The greedy seeker for power who, like Tamburlaine, makes use of others as footstools from which to ascend his throne, excites a general condemnation: and, however much he may secretly be admired, the ruthless man is more likely to invite criticism than to command respect.

But the less assertive person who identifies himself with others is often commended, although it is equally impossible to have a relationship with him. To be compliant, to abrogate one's own wishes and to fit in with the desires of others even at one's own expense—how admirable, how unselfish, how "Christian!" It is difficult for those who have been reared in the odour of sanctity to perceive that an undue submissiveness is as culpable as an undue assertiveness, and that maturity demands a relationship on equal terms. In his concept of maturity Fairbairn includes the genital relationship, which, as I have already remarked, is the touchstone of maturity for many psycho-analysts. But, for Fairbairn,[5] maturity in interpersonal relationship, while it includes the possibility of genital relationship between the sexes, implies more than this:

> At the same time, it must be stressed that it is not in virtue of the fact that the genital level has been reached that object-relationships are satisfactory. On the contrary, it is in virtue of the fact that satisfactory object-relationships have been established that true genital sexuality is attained.

And in a footnote to this extension of conventional psycho-analytic concepts he adds:

> It should be explained that it is not any part of my intention to depreciate the significance of the "genital" stage in comparison with the oral stage. My intention is rather to point out that the real significance of the "genital" stage lies in a *maturity of object-relationships*, and that a genital attitude is but an element in that maturity.

Throughout his writings, Fairbairn is concerned with persons as whole persons, not simply as vehicles for instinct. He reiterates that a child's basic need is to be loved "as a person." Writing of the origin of schizoid and depressive states he says:[6] "The traumatic situation in either case is one in which the child feels that he is not really loved as a person, and that his own love is not accepted."

But it is far from easy to describe what it is to love anyone as a person: and I think that both Jung and Fairbairn are showing that they find it difficult in the quotations given above, although it is abundantly clear that both know from experience the relationship that they are trying to delineate, and that they are convinced of its value.

Fairbairn postulates an initial stage in which the infant is both completely dependent upon, and completely identified with, its object, the mother. Progress towards maturity in relationship consists of a gradual differentiation of subject and object.[7] "Normal development is characterized by a process whereby progressive differentiation of the object is accompanied by a progressive decrease in identification." In other words, the more an individual becomes a separate individual in his own right, the more is he able to regard others as separate individuals in their own right.

Writers vary in how they describe the psychological journey towards maturity. Some, like Jung, are chiefly concerned with dynamic changes within the individual; others, like Fairbairn, depict his changing relationships with other individuals. But if one searches the pages of Jung one finds that he describes maturity also in terms of interpersonal relationships: and Fairbairn can be found to paint a picture of changing intrapsychic dynamics. It is clear that the development of the individual and the development of his relationships proceed *pari passu*; and that the one cannot take place without the other. In the analytic process, which, I believe, is a microcosm reflecting the macrocosm of the patient's relationships in the world outside the consulting room, the changing relationship to the analyst and the changing dynamics of the patient can be observed to occur as part of the same process.

One aspect of maturity in relationship seems to be, therefore, the avoidance of either dominating or being dominated by the other person. But, since men are by no means equal, it may be argued that such relationship could never occur: since it is impossible to conceive of a relationship between two people in which one would not be superior to the other in at least one facet of his endowment or achievement. Erich Fromm,[8] in *The Fear of Freedom*, answers this argument as follows:

> The uniqueness of the self in no way contradicts the principle of equality. The thesis that men are born equal implies that they all share the same fundamental qualities, that they share the basic fate of human beings, that they all have the same in-

alienable claim on freedom and happiness. It fur-
thermore means that their relationship is one of
solidarity, not one of domination-submission. What
the concept of equality does not mean is that all
men are alike. Such a concept of equality is derived
from the role that the individual plays in his economic activities today. In the relation between the
man who buys and the one who sells, the concrete
differences of personality are eliminated. In this situation only one thing matters, that the one has
something to sell and the other has money to buy
it. In economic life one man is not different from
another; as real persons they are, and the cultivation
of their uniqueness is the essence of individuality.

It is unfortunate that Fromm should use the phrase "the
thesis that men are born equal." It is abundantly clear that
they are not, and, although Fromm goes on to define this
quality in terms which indicate that he does not mean what
he says, it is a pity that he chooses these words. Men are
not born equal; but they share the human condition and,
however disparate their genetic endowment, however great
their inequality, they still have in common the fact that
they are human beings, and they are linked emotionally by
this fact. Moreover, the possibility of maturation is not confined to the highly gifted: and most of us have probably known
individuals of humble social position and limited intelligence
who have nevertheless impressed us as personalities in their
own right with their own individual style of life.

Disparity of endowment by no means precludes, although it may make more difficult, the kind of relationship
which I should call mature; just as disparity of social background may be a hindrance but is not a bar to a happy

marriage. The psychotherapist is in an especially favourable position to appreciate this, since he is usually fortunate enough to get to know intimately people of vastly different backgrounds and endowments, both superior and inferior to his own, and thus may have a wider circle of close acquaintances than do men in other professions. Much of our daily intercourse with people is regulated by convention; and we often fail to treat the people with whom we have dealings as individuals in their own right. The shopkeeper is the shopkeeper, the doctor a doctor—not a person, but simply an impersonal function or skill which we happen to need at the time. We do not know these people as individuals, and indeed might be surprised if we knew the person who lay behind the social role. Even apparently intimate relationships can be of this impersonal kind; and many sexual encounters are examples of meetings in which the man is a man and the woman a woman, and neither knows more or wishes to know more about the other than that. But the psychotherapist is daily confronted with problems of relationship in which he and the patient face each other as people, and in which the social role is of no importance. Any psychotherapist with experience will know that, when he has got to know a patient really well, there occur moments of recognition in which both he and the patient feel that some new insight, some area of truth, has been seen by each other. In such moments the barriers are down, the veils of concealment melt, and two people face each other just as they are, without fear and without pretence. There is no longer any question of superiority and inferiority; of dominance or submission; of intelligence or dullness; of giving or taking. Rather is there the recognition of the other as a personality, and therefore of oneself: of oneself and therefore of the other.

CHAPTER 4

THE DEVELOPMENT
OF PERSONALITY

*For I was: I was alive: I could feel: I could guard my
personality, the imprint of that mysterious unity from
which my being was derived.* ST. AUGUSTINE[1]

In the preceding chapter an attempt has been made to delineate the characteristics of a mature relationship, and the
hypothesis that the development of the individual and the
development of his relationship with others are inseparably
linked has been propounded. It has already been pointed
out, and may here be emphasized, that such a concept of
maturity of personality and of interpersonal relationships is
an ideal which is never wholly attained; for the development of personality seems to be a continuous process which
is never completed.

This is one reason why analytical treatment may go on
interminably: there is no good reason to stop, since development is always proceeding. This is a subject to which I
shall revert when discussing analysis as a maturing agent.
Ideals are always suspect, and the blind pursuit of them
frequently leads to destruction. But if we are to have a
coherent scheme of the development of personality some
concept of maturity is inevitable, and this is bound to be
in some sense "ideal" if the postulate that the development
of personality is never complete is accepted, as I think it
must be. A concept of maturity, however, presupposes a

concept of immaturity; and here we run into difficulties. The development of personality must obviously have a beginning as well as the end which we have attempted to sketch above; but, unfortunately, the beginnings of personality are shrouded in obscurity. In dealing with adults the distorting mirror of our subjective scheme may reflect back to us only our own psychopathology; but at least the patient can protest, and if our interpretations fail to fit his material or illumine his difficulties he can rise up in wrath and tell us so. But, in considering the small child, subjective prejudice has no limit. Speculation can be unconfined, and the baby is unable to argue with our concepts of his inner world. We may, perhaps, take comfort once again from physics. It has been necessary to construct mental pictures, imaginary models of the atom in order to understand the behaviour of atoms. No one has ever seen an atom, but they can be weighed, their behaviour can be predicted, and they can even be transformed, as we know to our cost. Various pictures of the atom have been constructed, each incomplete, each imperfect, but each stimulating observation and research which has led to new discoveries and, correspondingly, to modifications in the original picture. The mind of the baby is as inaccessible as the interior of the atom to direct observation; but some sort of scheme is necessary if we are to be able to make valid observations about infantile behaviour or to understand those persistent emotional reactions in adult life which we call immature, and which seem to be one foundation of neurotic symptoms.

The predominant belief which many workers appear to share, and with which I find myself in sympathy, is that at the beginning of its existence the child is a unity, undivided against itself, harmonious and, in a certain sense, integrated. The assumption is that, in the natural state of affairs, the baby has no problems, and that it is only in the course of its development towards adulthood that the difficulties arise. We have already postulated an ideal final state, a state of maturity which appears to be the end of human striving; now we postulate an ideal initial state, from which the child has necessarily to emerge. It is the transition between the two which gives rise to difficulties and tribulation.

Just where this ideal state is to be found is a matter of controversy; and some writers believe that the process of birth necessarily terminates the idyllic unity of the child by separating it from the mother within whom it has hitherto been contained. Others believe that the child finds all that it needs at the breast of the mother, and that the satisfaction which succeeds the act of suckling is the prototype of all later satisfaction, so that the idyllic conflict-free state will never again be attained till genital primacy and a satisfactory contrasexual partner has been won.*

It is amusing, and may be instructive, to note that similar ideas were current three centuries before Christ.[3]

> For Tao is itself the always-so, the fixed, the unconditioned, that which "is to itself" and for no cause "so." In the individual it is the Uncarved Block, the consciousness on which no impression has been "notched," in the universe it is the Primal Unity underlying apparent multiplicity. Nearest then to Tao is the infant. . . .

---

*"Satisfaction at the breast is the unattainable prototype of every later satisfaction" (Freud).[2]

The author adds in a footnote that the idea of the infant being nearest to Tao "was probably one that did not become popular till about 300 B.C. In the early centuries of the Christian era, on the other hand, it is no longer the infant but the child in the womb that is the Taoist ideal." Even Freud and Rank have their precursors.

We are here dealing with a mythology, a hypothetical construct; but such a construct is necessary if we are to understand the development of the individual, and, however reluctant we may be to adopt a theory which cannot be confirmed by direct observation, any scheme of development demands not only an end but also a beginning.

Some analysts would claim that the material produced by adult patients in analysis is reliable evidence of the earliest stages of infantile development; but such material, like dreams, is susceptible of different interpretations and thus can be made to fit different theoretical schemes. We must, I think, be content to accept the fact that our pictures are only pictures; and eschew dogmatism in a field which is bound to be speculative. What we need here is a comparative psychopathology: a serious study of all the varying points of view propounded by writers in the development of personality. This would be a formidable task and cannot be attempted here. But even a brief examination of three different writers reveals a similarity of conception which is interesting.

Freud[4] regarded instincts as being divided into two groups—"erotic instincts, which are always trying to collect living substances together into ever larger unities, and the death instincts, which act against that tendency and try to bring living matter back into an inorganic condition. The cooperation and opposition of these two forces produces the phenomena of life to which death puts an end." He recognized, and indeed stated, that this concept was a mythology.[5] "The instincts are mythical beings, superb in their indefiniteness." At first sight it would appear that Freud therefore postulated an innate state of conflict from the beginning, a primal opposition between love and hate. But in a later passage in this same paper he says[6]

> We recognize two fundamental instincts, and ascribe to each of them its own aim. How the two mingle in the vital process, how the death instinct is pressed into the service of Eros, especially when it is turned outwards in the form of aggressiveness— these are problems which remain for future investigation. We can go no further than the point at which this prospect opens up before us. The question whether all instincts without exception do not possess a conservative character, whether the erotic instincts also do not seek *the reinstatement of an earlier state of things*, when they strive towards the synthesis of living substances into larger wholes—this question too must be left unanswered.

And, in another passage, Freud says:[7]

> We may picture an initial state of things by supposing that the whole available energy of Eros, to which we shall henceforth give the name of Libido, is present in the as yet undifferentiated ego-id and serves to neutralize the destructive impulses which are simultaneously present.

The views of Melanie Klein are put forward by Money-Kyrle[8] later as follows:

The fact that in reality the first object, the mother's breast, is sometimes satisfying and sometimes frustrating, in itself tends to initiate such splits. But this may not be their only cause. What later appear as the opposite emotions of protective love and destructive hate may be by no means simple representations of two externally opposing groups of instincts. To a great extent they may originate in one confused and violent desire which is inherently unstable because in its very greed it threatens to destroy what it would most ardently preserve.

This seems to be an advance on Freud's conception. Fairbairn's views are still further advanced, as I see it. Fairbairn also conceives of an initial unity which he calls a "central ego." This is[9] "conceived as a primary and dynamic structure, from which, as we shall shortly see, the other mental structures are subsequently derived." From this central ego is derived a pair of opposites which Fairbairn at first called the "libidinal ego" and the "internal saboteur"; he later changed the name of the latter to "anti-libidinal ego." In his paper on hysterical states Fairbairn gives a synopsis of his views in which he says:[10] "The pristine personality of the child consists of a unitary dynamic ego."

It seems to me that these views are a developmental series. Freud postulates a basic conflict with two instincts fundamentally opposed to one another but with a remote possibility there might be a unity prior to this.

Money-Kyrle goes a little further and postulates a more definite unity, albeit an extremely unstable one.

Fairbairn is much more specific, and postulates a unity of a very definite kind before his pair of opposites is split off. This is, of course, a recurrent theme in the views of human nature propounded by men other than psychotherapists. The views of Rousseau, the second chapter of Genesis, the beliefs of many primitive peoples, attest the necessity of men conceiving their development in terms of a lost Age of Innocence or perfect state—a condition prior to the knowledge of good and evil. I say "the necessity" advisedly, for it seems a limitation of the human mind that we have to think in terms of time; and I cannot conceive of a scheme of human development which would not have a beginning, a middle, and an end—even though both beginning and end might still have something hypothetical about them; that is, be logical extensions of the theories which are necessary to explain our observations of the here and now—just as the existence or, it may be, the former existence of a distant star is necessary to explain the light which we see from it this evening, although so many "light years" intervene between the star and the earth that it may have ceased to exist long ago.

The concept of the death instinct is rejected by most psychopathologists; but, whatever we may think of this, a dichotomy between love and hate or good and bad is inescapable; and the psychotherapist, whatever school he may belong to, is bound to be faced with the problem of aggression at some stage in his thought. There are two main schools of opinion. One school, with a sombre regard for the actual state of the world, propounds the view that aggression is primary and instinctive; that men are inescapably bound to be hostile and destructive; and that, while love and affection are certainly preferable to hate and violence, the actions of men are as much influenced by the less as by the more desirable group of propensities.

The other school, more hopefully and, some would say,

too idealistically, proposes that aggression arises only in response to frustration: and that men only exhibit hate and violence in so far as their loving impulses have been rejected or in some way blocked. They recognize that every human being is frustrated to some extent, and therefore manifests a certain degree of aggression: but they feel that, if the development stages of infancy and childhood were attended with that completeness of loving acceptance which the child requires, aggressiveness would be reduced to a minimum and, in ideal circumstances, would disappear altogether.

In considering this problem I am struck by the following considerations. Firstly, everyone agrees that the dichotomy between loving and hating, between "good" and "bad" or "exciting" and "rejecting" objects occurs extremely early in the child's existence—so early that one might be forgiven for saying that there was no objective evidence of it. Secondly, the further back in infantile development aggression is traced the more terrifyingly violent and destructive it becomes; the findings of Melanie Klein can only be matched by horror comics or Foxe's *Book of Martyrs*. Thirdly, although there is no limit to the sadistic horrors of which supposedly adult human beings are capable, it seems to be generally true under normal conditions of civilization that children are more aggressive to each other than adults, and that adults who have attained their ambitions are less aggressive in general than those who have not. Fourthly, dependence and aggression are indissolubly linked; for to be dependent upon another person implies some degree of restriction by that person. Restriction, as one form of frustration, evokes aggression; and thus the child is inevitably bound to want to bite the hand that feeds it. The hand that rocks the cradle erects the play-pen; and, whilst security is given on the one hand, restriction is imposed upon the other, with the result that all parents are bound to be ambivalent figures and to excite both love and hatred in their offspring.

If this historical view of aggression is taken, it will be seen that it can be postulated that aggressiveness is both innate and likely to become progressively less important as development proceeds. Aggression is necessary for development, for separateness, for the achievement of differentiation from the parents. Competitive aggressiveness, sibling rivalry, is characteristic of immaturity and should diminish as self-realization proceeds. It is futile to expect a millennium of brotherly love to occur, even if every living being had an ideally secure childhood; but there is some reason to suppose that aggressive tensions can be lessened if the grosser inequalities between peoples can be diminished. Aggressiveness is at its maximum when dependence (and hence inequality) is at its maximum; as development proceeds it becomes less important till, at the point of maximum development, only so much aggression exists as is necessary to maintain the personality as a separate entity.

Development is often impeded by the immaturity of parents, and it is true to say that the less a parent is mature the less can he tolerate rebellion in his children, and the more does he require their subservience and their agreement with him. Neurotic, insecure parents tend to have neurotic, insecure children; and it is largely because immature parents cannot tolerate differentiation from themselves that this is so. But differentiation is essential for individuality; two people who share the same views, hold the same opinions, and have the same interests are not differentiated but identified; and the wish of parents that their children should be like them is a narcissistic one. They want to hold a mirror to themselves and see that what they have created is both good and in their own image. The notion that it is always wrong or dangerous to oppose anyone else is easily implanted in the child, but the behaviour which such a notion imposes is crippling to the personality as a whole, for individuality implies opposition and differentiation.

It has already been emphasized that, if men are to achieve mature relationships on equal terms, submission to another person is as undesirable as domination of that person. Unfortunately, we have no word which describes the middle way between these two opposites—and most terms which we employ carry emotional overtones of condemnation. A certain opposition to others in adult life is necessary if the personality is to be maintained as a separate entity; and this is clearly connected with the aggressive impulses which are characteristic of childhood; but to use the word "aggression" in connexion with the dignity and independence of the mature personality is to create a wrong impression. All affirmation of the personality is "aggressive"—but there is no word which conveys the idea of aggression without hostility, which is the concept I am trying to convey.

It seems to me that maturity is characterized by assertion and affirmation of the personality without hostility and without competitiveness, both of which characteristics are typical of childhood. The more a man has succeeded in realizing his own personality, the less compulsion will he feel to be competitive and the less hostile will he be to others. Men are very differently endowed; and the maturity of the man with an I.Q. of 80 will be very different from that of the man with an I.Q. of 140; but, provided each can make full use of his differing endowments, there is no reason why each should not be equally at peace with himself and with his neighbour. Common experience bears witness to the fact that it is the people who have least succeeded in realizing their own potentialities who are the most hostile, and that the best way of dealing with a rebel is often to put him in a position of authority.

Most psychotherapists are struck by the alternation of "love" and "hate" in the personality and put forward varying points of view about this dichotomy. Extreme oscillation between love and hate, especially of the same person, is characteristic of childhood, since the most important relationship of childhood, that with the parents, is one in which the loved object is bound to be restrictive, and hence also resented. In adult life the loved object is, at any rate ideally, cooperative rather than restrictive; and hence can be loved unconditionally without the admixture of hate, though every man is aware that this is an ideal, since at times he is bound to treat his wife as a mother—and she to treat him as a father.

Adults sometimes want to go back to childhood, and most of those who do have repressed the vicissitudes and pains of that period of their lives. "Old boys" who hanker after a return to school are indeed "boys" emotionally; and it is their failure to attain any more mature relationship which prompts their wish to regress. Nevertheless, small children exert a fascination which is both universal and psychologically interesting; and I suggest that, under some circumstances, children do possess something valuable which is lost as they grow up, which may never be regained in adult life, and which therefore excites both nostalgia and admiration in adults who have to do with them.

Historically, our attitudes to children have varied. At times they have been treated like adults; at other times secluded in nurseries. We are, perhaps, still inclined to the sentimentalization of the child so characteristic of the late Victorian era, which Freud disturbed by his emphasis on infantile sexuality; and the financial success of campaigns on behalf of children demonstrates their superiority to adults in emotional appeal. Children are far from being little angels, and their "innocence" is not what it was thought to be in pre-Freudian times; but, nevertheless, most adults have at times been charmed by small children and have a special attitude towards them. It is of interest to inquire in what their charm consists.

At the very beginning of life the baby is usually accepted without conditions, and there is now some evidence that those which are not so accepted suffer in later life as a result. Babies are what they are, and are not generally expected to be anything else. Crumpled, red, vociferous, and incontinent, they are yet wonderful to their mothers, and whatever they do is accepted. Although those of us who cannot be mothers may never be able to manifest this entire devotion, we have all at times admired the spontaneity, unaffectedness, and *joie de vivre* of small children. Children are also excessively demanding, require constant attention, and are far from always exhibiting the sort of behaviour which we find endearing; but given the right conditions, they show a freedom of expression and an unaffected naturalness which we as adults may envy; for we can no longer display it. This freedom of the child is, of course, only possible in a sheltered environment in which it feels at ease. The intrusion of a stranger may break the spell, and it is probably only parents or parent surrogates who see the child behaving in a completely uncomplicated way. Children need a playground of emotional security if they are to be most surely themselves and behave in the unsophisticated, naïve, and charming manner which elicits our delight in them.

If I am right in thinking that it is the spontaneity and

freedom which children can exhibit which constitutes their appeal, it is not difficult to see why there seems to be a connexion, a similarity, between the two extremes of immaturity and maturity. As the child develops, its spontaneity and freedom grows less, for it is bound to come into conflict with parents and other authorities; and in its efforts to adapt, to be what it conceives others want it to be, to fit in with society, it must necessarily leave behind the idyllic state of completeness with which we postulate that it started and of which traces can still be seen under the conditions suggested above. But, as development proceeds, the lost freedom of childhood is replaced by the new freedom of maturity, and the security of the accepted child may once again be attained in the achievement of a fully adult relationship with others.

The wish to return to childhood is, in most instances, a regressive wish—a desire to abrogate adult responsibilities and to return to a state of dependence. But this wish may also have another aspect. To seek after the spontaneity and freedom of the secure child is a different matter and may, perhaps, be what is meant in the saying of Christ:[11] "Except ye be converted and become as little children ye shall not enter into the Kingdom of heaven." This is no regression to childishness, but rather an advance to such security and freedom with our fellow-men that we can be whatever we are and allow them to be the same.

CHAPTER 5

THE EMERGENT PERSONALITY

The most that we can hope to do is to train every individual to realize all his potentialities and become completely himself. ALDOUS HUXLEY[1]

A good deal of fruitless controversy takes place between those who consider that personality is predominantly the result of environmental influences and those who believe that it is chiefly determined by the inherited genetic endowment. Psycho-analysis, while never denying that men differ innately, has laid so much emphasis upon real or hypothetical influences in early childhood that some psychiatrists have felt that the genetic factors in the personality were being undervalued, and that psycho-analysts assumed that a silk purse could be made out of every sow's ear if only the analysis were deep enough in extent and prolonged enough in time. On the other hand, genetic research is so complicated, and has progressed so little, that it remains impossible to say in the majority of cases of persons with psychiatric disorders how far the disorder is related to genetic and how far to environmental causes. Diseases such as Huntington's chorea, in which a single dominant gene is responsible, are the exception rather than the rule, and it is generally agreed that the inheritance of most human characteristics is multifactorial. One has only to consider in how very few instances of mental disorder one is justified

53

in advising against reproduction upon eugenic grounds; how little evidence there really is for the widespread belief that certain types of neurosis are "constitutional" in origin; how inadequate our knowledge of *what* is actually inherited, to realize that, however shaky our psycho-dynamic concepts may be, our genetic knowledge is still shakier. A recent textbook[2] of psychiatry, of which one of the co-authors is the leading expert on psychiatric genetics in this country, states of the manic-depressive psychosis:

> To summarize the present state of our knowledge, we may say that the significance of hereditary factors in the causation of manic-depressive psychoses is established. The mode of inheritance tends to take a dominant form, but the gene-carriers develop the psychosis in only a minority of cases. The effect of non-genital factors has to be taken into account. Finally, the relative importance of single specific and of multifactorial genes, and the degree of genetical hetero-geneity, are still unclarified.

In other words, although "the significance of hereditary factors . . . is established," prediction of any accurate kind is impossible; one can carry the gene without developing the disorder, and no one can tell which of the vast population carrying the gene is likely to develop it. The *presence* of hereditary factors may have been demonstrated, but it seems premature to say that their *significance* has been established until some clearer statement can be made as to their relative importance compared with factors in the environment.

It is clear that it is easier to predict the character structure of a child reared in certain specific ways than it is to foretell his future from his ancestry. Even if both his parents are manic-depressive, and their parents, and their parents before them, it would not be safe to bet upon his becoming manic-depressive. But, if he is separated from his mother in infancy and then persistently ill-treated, if he is reared in fear and cowed and beaten, his adult character may be compounded of variable degrees of fear and hatred—and it is safe to say that both those attributes will exist as part of his adult personality in extreme measure. Let us revert to the textbook of psychiatry[3] and see what the authors have to say of schizophrenia:

> Our knowledge of the genetics of schizophrenia provides the basis for some conclusions about prophylaxis. These conclusions are, however, best expressed in terms of probabilities, and provide no certainty in the individual case. . . . The incidence of schizophrenia among the children of schizophrenics is between 10 and 20 per cent depending on the type of psychosis. So it might be expected that sterilizing schizophrenics would prevent the birth of a substantial number of persons destined later to develop the disease. Schizophrenics, however, have a very low fertility, and, of such children as they do have, only a small proportion are born after the onset of the psychosis—that is, after the schizophrenic has become recognizable as such. The great majority of schizophrenics are the children of non-schizophrenic parents. And in fact the sterilization of schizophrenics is almost useless as a prophylactic measure.

It appears from these quotations that so little is yet known about the genetics of even the major psychoses that to attribute an overwhelming importance to genetic factors in the causation of mental disorder is as yet premature; and, although one may hope that future research in genetics may illumine the study of personality and mental disorder, the present contribution of genetic knowledge is extremely small. It is reasonable to argue the schizophrenic parents are as likely to produce schizophrenic offspring because of the way they treat their children, as because of the genes which they transmit to them; and gross instances of neglect and ill-treatment of children are not infrequently the result of schizophrenia in the mother. It is generally agreed that in most cases of schizophrenia schizoid character traits can be detected in the pre-psychotic personality; so that, even if children are born prior to the onset of the psychosis, it is reasonable to assume that there will have been a certain lack of emotional warmth and security in their early environment which may well predispose them in their turn to a schizophrenic breakdown in early adult life. At our present stage of knowledge it is premature to argue that either the genetic factor or the effect of the early emotional environment is supreme, and it is unfortunate that those who are engaged in genetic research have so little experience in psycho-therapy, and that psychotherapists know so little of genetics. The admirable desire for scientific certainty, for a firm basis for research, and for a yard-stick by which genetic factors can be separated from other factors, provides the basis for a belief in the importance of genetics which is certainly as emotionally determined as is the belief in the overwhelming importance of the early emotional environment. A further quotation from the same textbook[4] may serve to illustrate this. Referring to schizophrenia, the authors go on:

The universal incidence of the disease in all races and cultures weighs heavily against any arguments that environmental and psychological factors of any specific kind play an important part in causing the disease; and so does the experience of the clinician who sees identical clinical pictures in patients from all walks of life and from the most diverse family and educational backgrounds. The dangers of being misled by facile optimism are exemplified by a patient known to us, who was adopted as a child by a woman psychiatrist and brought up in the most favourable circumstances by methods derived from his mother's great experiences in analytical psychopathology. He nevertheless developed after puberty a simple schizophrenia, changed school several times, and finally had to be admitted to a hospital for treatment.

But the facts that schizophrenia is of universal occurrence and that the patients suffering from it are very much alike, are really not evidence against environmental and psychological factors. Men suffering from extreme anger are also very much alike, behave in the same way, and can be found daily anywhere in the world. It is hardly to be supposed, however, that anger is for this reason genetically determined and not at all the result of environmental and psychological factors of a specific kind. Schizophrenia is generally a chronic condition, whilst anger is usually transitory; but it is equally a human reaction and not a disease. Every effort to prove that schizophrenia is a disease in the sense that general paralysis of the insane is a disease has so far failed. It is surely time that this way of looking at schizoophrenia was dropped, and that it was recognized as a mode of reaction of the personality which is latent in all of us.

It is only comparatively recently that it has been recognized that everyone is liable to epilepsy. Some people will have an epileptic fit only if an electric current is applied to their brain or they are given an intravenous injection of leptazol. Other people may react with a fit to minor stimuli of various kinds, while still others have fits apparently spontaneously. Just as some people require a major physiological stimulus to produce a fit, so some need isolation and mescaline to produce a schizophrenic condition.

Others may be so constituted that it requires only very moderate adversity to cause their psyche to disintegrate; and, although twin studies show a very high incidence of schizophrenia in uniovular partners, it is also true to say that[5] "some of the uniovular partners of schizophrenics not only did not develop schizophrenia, but showed no noteworthy psychiatric abnormality."

We need to know not so much what causes schizophrenia but what prevents it. The universality of the disorder and the similarity of the symptoms attest the basic similarity of the human psyche; but this is scarcely evidence that schizophrenia is dependent of any external factors. In the example given above the authors do not tell us at what age the child was adopted. It is a tenable, though unproven, hypothesis that the tendency to become schizophrenic is related to emotional damage at an early age—and the early environment of a child who has later to be adopted is unlikely to be favourable. Moreover, the authors show an excessive naïveté when they assume that because the adopting mother is a psychiatrist with "great experience in analytical psychopathology" the child will be brought up in "the most favourable circumstances." Even the least sophisticated of

psychotherapists will usually admit that he became interested in psychotherapy because of his own emotional problems; and that, although his psychopathological insight may
have given him the ability to handle human problems in
a constructive way, he is no better equipped to bring up
children than a completely unsophisticated person who
loves his children unthinkingly and who would never dream
of consulting a book or a psychiatrist on how to bring
them up.

People are not attacked by schizophrenia as by influ-
enza; they regress or relapse into it; and, although many
cases of the disorder appear to be irreversible, striking instances of the temporary "recovery" of the most chronic
cases are known to every psychiatrist. No organic pathology
of a definite kind has ever been demonstrated in schizophrenia; but it is comparatively easy to demonstrate that
the schizophrenic condition is improved by any attempt at
making a relationship with the patient. The more attention
that is given to schizophrenics in hospital the less deteriorated, the less "schizophrenic," do they become; and the
increasing use of occupational therapy for patients who have
been mentally ill for many years has resulted in a considerable change in the behavior and appearance of those in
the chronic wards of the mental hospitals. The mute, incontinent, cyanosed, oedematous schizophrenic is rarer than
he was, and in time he may disappear altogether. Schizophrenia seems to be a failure of the personality to cohere
as a whole, and this failure of inner cohesion is reflected in
the outer absence of relationships which is the most striking
feature of schizophrenia. In his *Introductory Lectures on
Psycho-Analysis* Freud[6] says: "Already in 1908, K. Abraham
expressed the view after a discussion with me that the main
characteristic of dementia praecox (reckoned as one of the

psychoses) is that in this disease the investments of objects with libido is lacking.'' It is as if one was talking to a series of complexes or mental processes, not to a person; as if one was presented with all the parts of the body dissected from each other with no unity to bind them into a single body. Schizophrenia will continue to be a mystery so long as we fail to understand the forces and the organization which make for the wholeness of personality. It seems to be an essentially negative condition in which something is lacking, and in which "personality" in the sense of individuality is lost. The similarity of schizophrenic symptomatology and experience is good evidence for the hypothesis of the collective unconscious advanced by Jung; a level of physical functioning which is characterized by the recurrence of certain basic archetypal themes and in which individual personal psychological material is largely absent. Whatever views are held on this point, there can be no disputing the fact that schizophrenics improve if a personal interest is taken in them, and deteriorate if they are left alone. I find it helpful to think of schizophrenia as the very opposite of self-realization. It is the negation of personality, the absence of individuality, the disintegration as opposed to the integration of the whole person. It has recently been suggested that the comparative success of the insulin coma treatment of schizophrenia depends upon the fact that the treatment is difficult to administer and necessitates a good many people giving a great deal of attention over a long period to each patient. This may well be true. If it is right to assume that the most striking feature of schizophrenia is the emotional isolation of the patient, one would expect that any method of treatment which broke down this isolation would be at least partially effective.

It seems absurd that there should be any serious divergence between geneticists and psychopathologists, for it is surely obvious that the development of personality is dependent both on heredity and environment, and that in seeking to evaluate which of the two factors is the most important we are probably trying to over-simplify something which is extremely complicated. It is clear that men differ widely; and probable that many of the differences between them are inborn and constitutional; but how far any particular characteristic is the product of early environmental conditioning and how far it is inherited as such is quite unknown. As an example, one might consider Jung's dichotomy of introversion—extraversion; a classification which has appeared even more valuable to psychologists and research workers than to psychotherapists. Jung himself seems to regard his types as predominantly constitutional in origin, not the result of infantile emotional experience. Fairbairn also recognizes two basic types which he calls schizoid and depressive, which he recognizes as being similar to Jung's; but, although admitting hereditary factors, he attributes the differences between the types predominantly to infantile experience.

My own working hypothesis is that personality is indeed genetically determined, but that the extent to which each personality reaches maturity, fruition, and realization is largely dependent upon environmental factors. The seed contains the promise of the future plant, and nothing will make oranges grow from plum stones, or plums from orange pips; but the soil and climate which encourage the orange may be too exotic for the plum, and the orange will find too rigorous conditions in which the plum may flourish.

It seems to me inescapable that men are profoundly different in constitution; and it requires an exceptional capacity of detachment and toleration for the psychotherapist to treat people who may be poles apart from himself in temperament and outlook. It is, however, one of the rewards of an exacting profession that the psychotherapist gets to know intimately people who are very differently constituted from himself; and although no one's sympathies can be universal, yet it is probable that those of the psychotherapist become wider rather than narrower as he himself matures.

The most extensive contemporary investigation into human constitution has been that of Sheldon,[7] whose concepts of mesomorphy, endomorphy, and ectomorphy with their temperamental equivalents of somatotonia, viscerotonia, and cerebrotonia are becoming increasingly widely adopted. Sheldon and his associates have advanced the interesting suggestion that neurosis is due to the unavailing struggle of people to be something different from that to which their constitutional endowment would naturally incline them. Sheldon believes that physique and character are intimately related; and anyone who has studied his writings and those of Kretschmer[8] must be impressed with the case they put forward, although proof is at present lacking. J. M. Tanner,[9] who has worked with Sheldon, admits in an interesting article that there is not yet very much confirmed scientific evidence in favour of a close relationship between physique and character. But he goes on to say:

> This admission places me in a quandary because I think that the evidence of everyday life is strongly in favour of the existence of a relationship, and of one very much of the sort described by Kretschmer and by Sheldon. I would go even further and say that I *think* that I see neurotic behaviour quite often coming from an attempt to behave in a fashion out

of character with what one might predict from the physique. I think I see more often than by chance neurotic traits diminishing as the person concerned comes to act more in accordance with theoretical expectation.

The idea that men can act, so to speak, out of character and that they become neurotic if they do so seems to me a very valuable one. If this hypothesis is accepted it is implied that a man can also reach some sort of solution to his problems by learning more about himself and acting more in accordance with his own nature. Jung has long held the view that the psyche is self-regulating, and that neurotic symptoms are not just unpleasant disturbances to be got rid of, but are also attempts on the part of the psyche to restore equilibrium. The view of neurosis put forward above by Tanner seems to contain the same idea.

One of the common objections to psychodynamic concepts of the causation of mental illness is the fact that, in a given family, one child may develop such an illness whereas another does not. Assuming that the environment and the type of upbringing has remained more or less constant, the argument is that genetic factors must be all-important. Of course it can be argued that no two children have exactly the same upbringing; that position in the family is important; that early experiences of feeding difficulties may be decisive and quite different for two children in the same family, and all this may be true. Nevertheless, the objection remains, and it is foolish to deny the importance of inherited constitution. But one child's meat may be another child's poison, and, whereas parental attitudes and temperaments may encourage the development of one child's personality, they may inhibit that of another child who happens to be differently endowed. In psychotherapy we are constantly dealing with the *interaction* between child and parent; with a relative, not an absolute, situation. The same parents may take on one aspect when seen through the eyes of an introverted child, and quite another when described by his more extraverted brother; and both descriptions may be "true" in that what is being described is not the actual personality of the parents, but the interaction between them and the child. I believe that it is ultimately possible to describe another person objectively, but only if one has been able to form with them that relationship which, in an earlier chapter, I have called mature; and, by definition, such a relationship cannot exist between child and parents while the child is still young. When patients describe the restrictions imposed upon them by their parents, the disapproval with which their struggle to assert themselves was attended, the guilt with which their emergent sexuality was surrounded, I take their description as being the truth for them but not as the truth which would be seen by an outside observer. A train travelling at fifty miles an hour may seem to be going fast if I am standing on the station platform, but if I am gradually passing it in a train going at seventy miles an hour I shall be impressed not by its speed by its sluggishness. The same train going at the same speed can appear slow on one occasion, fast on another; and both descriptions of its behaviour are "true," relative to the different circumstances of the observer. Anyone who has worked in a child-guidance clinic will have noticed that the parents as seen by the staff of the clinic are very often extremely different from the parents as seen by the child; and fathers and mothers who appear to the staff to be no more than normally solicitous may be regarded by the child as monstrously restrictive.

Analysts of every school are so often criticized for blaming the parents for subsequent neuroses of their children that it is worth labouring the point that the stresses and strains of development cannot be regarded objectively, but only through the eyes of the patient whose difficulties are none the less real because another person, differently constituted, might not have found them difficulties at all.

Environment is both very important, and also relative—which is why schemes of education, advice to parents, and psychological textbooks are of comparatively little use. There seems to me to be only one definite statement one can make about bringing up children—and that is that they should be accepted as individuals in their own right and their differences from their parents and each other tolerated and encouraged. Children develop most satisfactorily if they are loved for what they are, not for what anyone thinks they ought to be.

It seems probable that this irrational acceptance, this sense of being loved as a whole without reservation, is the basis of adult confidence in oneself as a person, and also of satisfying relationships with others; and that neurotic disharmony occurs as a result of real or imagined lack of acceptance. Owing to the long period of human helplessness, the child is bound to have to conform with what it thinks its parents want it to be—for to be anything else is to court the withdrawal of their protecting love. And so the child may come to pretend to be what it is not on the one hand, and to deny what it is on the other.

These mechanisms of pretence and denial can be seen in every neurosis in the adult, and I believe that the type of neurosis is dependent upon which mechanism is predominant.

The concepts of pretence and denial are closely connected with introjection and projection; but whereas some psycho-analysts seem to regard the personality as largely built-up introjections, I would incline to Jung's view that the child has a discrete personality of its own from the beginning. I would therefore consider that both projection and introjection are defensive devices. The young child, owing to its weakness and dependence, cannot dare to be entirely itself unless its personality happens to coincide exactly with what it comes to believe is required of it; and, since no child can be wholly in this happy position, it is bound to shift from being simply itself towards being more like what it thinks the parents want.

This shift away from the positive state of being itself involves a partial identification with the parents and an introjection of their attitudes; and part of the process of becoming mature will consist of expelling from the personality those attitudes and modes of behaviour which have been introjected for reasons of security, but which do not necessarily belong to the person concerned as part of his own personality.

CHAPTER 6

IDENTIFICATION AND INTROJECTION

Just as everything serves some purpose or other, so man serves a purpose in the scheme of things and realizes his full nature in it. This is to develop his depth, or inborn capacities so far as he possibly can.   BOWRA[1]

The term identification, in common with most psychological expressions, is susceptible of more than one meaning. It is therefore important to define the sense in which the word is used. As I use the term, identification is a phenomenon in which subject and object are not differentiated from each other, but assumed to be the same, although the real situation is that they are different. In the chapter "Definitions" in *Psychological Types*, Jung[2] says:

> Identification is an estrangement of the subject from himself in favour of an object in which the subject is, to a certain extent, disguised. For example, identification with the father practically signifies an adoption of the ways and manners of the father, as though the son were the same as the father and not a separate individual. *Identification* is distinguished from *imitation* by the fact that identification is an *unconscious* imitation, whereas imitation is a conscious copying.

The view that the acceptance of other people as different, as existing as separate entities in their own right, is a criterion of a mature relationship has already been advanced; and it is clear that identification with another person is a bar to being able to have an adult relationship with them. I have already quoted Fairbairn's[3] statement that "Normal development is characterized by a process whereby progressive differentiation of the object is accompanied by a progressive decrease in identification." This is an admirable and succinct exposition of a basic psychological truth; and I believe that the decrease in identification and the increase in differentiation proceeds as long as the personality continues to develop. But Fairbairn omits to indicate the fact that the later stages of development are also characterized by identifications of various kinds which serve a positive function in the maturation of the personality; and, although such identifications may be temporary, they may serve to evoke qualities which might otherwise have remained latent, and thus play a valuable part in development. Identification can also be regarded as an aid to self-discovery, and is not merely a state of infancy which should be discarded.

The most primitive and elementary type of identification is that of the infant with its mother; and it seems justifiable to assume that the infant only gradually becomes aware of himself as having a separate existence from her who so recently contained him. In the beginning it seems that the infant's world is a solipsistic one, and people are treated entirely from the subjective point of view. That is, the small child treats people as being there solely to minister to its needs, and not at all as creatures having lives of their own. The baby usually goes to sleep when its needs are satisfied; and those who serve it may, from the baby's viewpoint, temporarily cease to exist, only to be raised again when hunger demands their revival.

We cannot know exactly how long the image of a loved or needed person persists after it has fulfilled its function of satisfying the baby's need; but modern opinion suggests that the time-span increases with age. We know that in early childhood any prolonged absence of the mother is likely to mean her total disappearance.

The small child cannot conceive of a person's continued existence if she is not there in the flesh to substantiate it. Bowlby,[4] for instance, distinguishes these main phases in the development of the child's capacity for human relationships:

> In broad outline, the following are the most important:
>
> (a) The phase during which the infant is in the course of establishing a relation with a clearly identified person—his mother; this is normally achieved by five or six months of age.
>
> (b) The phase during which he needs her as an ever-present companion; this usually continues until about his third birthday.
>
> (c) The phase during which he is becoming able to maintain a relationship with her in her absence. During the fourth and fifth years such a relationship can only be maintained in favourable circumstances and for a few days or weeks at a time; after seven or eight the relationship can be maintained, though not without strain, for periods of a year or more.

One can speculate as to how the infant becomes conscious of the mother as a separate person at all. Is it by the discovery of the boundaries of its own body that the baby divides itself from its environment? Or is it that, when a need is not immediately satisfied, some vague concept that an object other than itself is necessary to satisfy it arises? Perhaps both these mechanisms operate together. But we can perhaps disagree with Bowlby's phraseology in his first delineation. The infant may establish a relationship with a recurrently recognized person—his mother; but it seems highly doubtful whether she is "clearly identified." In adult life it is not rare to meet neurotics who still cannot distinguish between what they feel and what their mother feels, and who attribute to their mothers thoughts and even bodily sensations which, to an outside observer, have nothing to do with anyone but themselves. The infant can hardly be expected to identify anyone else clearly. It is an achievement even to recognize the same person again; and this may really be a recognition of expected pleasure—not a response to a person who is identified as such.

We know and expect that the love of a small child is "cupboard" love; and that we who look after it are going to be treated not as people with lives of our own, but simply as slaves who are there to serve the child, and who will be "loved" in so far as we fulfil its wishes, and "hated" in so far as we refuse them. The psycho-analytic concept of infantile omnipotence refers to the supposed subjective state of feeling of the infant in which the whole world seems to be centred round its wishes and subservient to its desires. Absolute dependence does indeed arouse the maximum response from others: and the complete helplessness of the infant is its most powerful weapon. It has only to cry and willing hands will tend it; to smile, and ecstatic voices will commend it; to belch, and comforting shoulders will support it. It is not surprising that the external fact of helplessness is matched by an internal sense of omnipotence, and that these two apparent incompatibles march thus hand in hand.

In adult life it is always the most helpless patients who make the most demands upon the therapist; and such patients are unconscious of the fact that they treat people as slaves who are there to serve them rather than as people with whom they could have cooperative relationships on equal terms. It is because they feel so far from being on equal terms that they can be so demanding—for they do not believe that they have anything to give to anyone, and so other people are treated simply as givers and not as receivers, with a consequent absence of any reciprocal relationship. Love is conceived as a one-way traffic by those who have been deprived of it: and, if one believes that one has nothing to give, the only possible relationship with another person is that of passive receptivity—in psycho-analytic terminology, the early oral stage of development.

The hypothesis seems inescapable that the infant's world consists originally simply of itself; itself not separated from the mother who tends it, nor from the blankets which cover it, nor from the air which it breathes, nor from the milk which it imbibes. In the beginning was the All and Everything, the wholeness which comes from total dependence, the wholeness which is only broken by the realization that, since every desire is not immediately fulfilled, there must be something external to the infant, who is therefore not whole but incomplete.

The Buddhist ideal of freedom from desire is a search for this original wholeness: since only if one is free from desire is one free from dependence; only if one no longer wants anything is one complete in oneself. In schizophrenia we can sometimes see what this solipsistic world of the infant is like. Jung[5] quotes a patient who had "the magnificent idea that the world was his picture-book, the pages of which he could turn at will. The proof was quite simple: he had only to turn round, and there was a new page for him to see." This is omnipotence in all its pristine glory. A patient of mine used to represent himself by drawing a circle. He had the fantasy of the circle expanding until it included the whole world, so that he and the whole world would be finally indistinguishable. He was a schizophrenic who was quite incompetent to deal with the world in fact, and whose helplessness in the face of reality was accurately balanced by the omnipotence which existed in his inner world of fantasy.

It is only gradually that the small child begins to be aware of himself as a separate entity, and at the same time to be aware of other people as separate also. It is probably that this loss of the original or *primary identification* with the mother takes place partly by means of the child becoming orientated in space through the discovery of the boundaries of its own body. To kick an object is to discover that there is both a self and a not-self. Frustration is therefore important in self-discovery—the frustration of finding that all wants are not immediately satisfied leads to the discovery that one is dependent upon others: the frustration of finding intransigent objects to the realization that one has physical limitations and that there is an external world with which one is not coexistent, and over which one's power is limited.

This realization of separateness leads, I believe, to anxiety and fear; for, in the infant, this realization is necessarily attended by the simultaneous realization of dependence and helplessness. The small child who becomes increasingly aware of its separate existence from the mother is also liable to realize the dangers attendant upon her departure. Parents sometimes notice that a child, hitherto secure, may begin to exhibit anxiety about being left. They wonder what they have done wrong: but often there is no particular external reason to account for the change. The anxiety which the child exhibits often goes hand in hand with an increase in aggressive behaviour—the tempers which are so common in the fourth and fifth years when the beginnings of independence make themselves manifest. One way of looking at the child's anxiety is to say that, unconsciously, it was afraid that its aggression had destroyed the parents; and this would perhaps be the orthodox psycho-analytic view. It is also of value to look upon the anxiety as being related to the beginning of the child's emergence as a separate individual. It is by means of its aggression that it separates from the parents—and so it is indeed the fear caused by aggression that is the cause of the child's anxiety: but this fear is more that of being abandoned than that the parents have been destroyed.

The more the mother becomes a separate person with a will of her own, not merely a source of supply to be tapped at will, the greater is the danger that she will disregard the needs or wishes of the child. If child and mother are still identified, the mother is treated by the child as part of itself and therefore partly subservient to its will: but directly the mother's separateness is realized her necessary support must become dubious. That such an identification can persist into adult life is attested by the almost daily clinical experience of seeing daughters who are about to leave the maternal roof to get married. In many instances the strong link between mother and daughter has been completely unconscious until the time of separation draws near. The daughter has considered the mother so much as part of herself and so little as a separate person that she has never conceived of life without her: and the realization that she is henceforward to be without her mother's support gives rise to fear. Many mothers encourage this unconsciousness on the part of their children by always doing everything for them, and thus never allowing the children to develop in their own right. The mother is then treating the child merely as an extension of her own personality and not as a person in its own right—and so herself ensures that the unconscious identity shall persist. In such cases the dependence of mother upon daughter is as great as that of daughter upon mother: and each fears abandonment by the other.

Throughout this book the hypothesis that human beings need each other for their own development has been adhered to; and the idea that maturity consists not so much in independence as in the achievement of a mature relationship with others has been underlined. It will therefore surprise no one who has so far followed my argument that I consider the fear of abandonment to be one of the basic fears of mankind. Even in adult life we are inescapably dependent upon each other for our mental health; and no one can accept emotional isolation and retain his personality intact. "To feel completely alone and isolated leads to mental disintegration just as physical starvation leads to death."[6] It is not therefore surprising that the child dreads the loss of those upon whom he is dependent—not only because of his physical needs, but also because the preservation of the developing structure of his personality depends upon a sustained relationship with people who accept him. That disintegration of personality and loss of object-relationships march together can be clearly seen in schizophrenia: and the fear of abandonment can be taken as being in essence equivalent to the fear of insanity.

The fear of being abandoned leads to an attempt to re-identify with the parents and to an introjection of their standards and attitudes—in other words, to the establishment of that internal and primitive type of conscience which psycho-analysis has made familiar as the super-ego. The small baby which is unconscious of its separateness may feel both omnipotent and secure so long as its actual helplessness is complete and the adults with whom it is surrounded minister at once to its needs. But directly it begins to be aware of itself as a separate individual, and adults are not so immediately ready to serve it, it becomes expedient for the child to try and please the adults for fear that they may abandon it or punish it. When in Rome it is safer to do as the Romans do, or one may arouse their wrath: and it is therefore expedient to assume the aspect, and mimic the behaviour, of those upon whose benevolence one's security depends.

One way, therefore, of dealing with the anxiety which the loss of primary identification inevitably entails is to introject the standards and attitudes of the parental figures and thus to re-identify with them. Such standards and attitudes may coincide with the inherited disposition of the child: and there are many men who go through life content to hold the beliefs and persist in the mode of existence which their forefathers have handed down to them. Others are destined to find their own way; to rebel against the traditions which have been transmitted to them; to suffer anxiety and the fear which attends separation from the parents; and, finally, to win their way to a new individual point of view. Such men are those whose genetic endowment makes it impossible for them to preserve the integrity of their own personalities and, at the same time, preserve the parental attitudes which they have introjected. They are compelled to fight their way to freedom; to find their own individual way of life; and to discard the traditions in which they have been reared. For such people self-realization consists partly in becoming conscious of, and subsequently discarding, introjected parental attitudes: and the earlier some degree of emotional security is attained, the sooner will this discarding take place. Emotional security is more likely to be attained in a household in which the parents are secure enough to be able to tolerate difference from themselves, and mature enough to make relationships with children who are not just little models of themselves, but individuals in their own right. It is only people who themselves need reassurance who have to insist that those around them conform to their own tastes and opinions; the ability to tolerate difference from oneself is a good test of maturity. Parents often treat children not as discrete entities but as parts of themselves, and become disturbed when they find that their children have separate interests and identities. It is my impression that the children who are most identified with their parents are those whose upbringing has been most fraught with anxiety; and, if they become patients in adult life, one can observe with what irrational fear even the smallest departure from parental standards is attended. To see the true personality trying to emerge and to cast off identifications which have been made solely on grounds of security is rewarding, and it is a process which is accompanied by a new firmness and certainty on the part of the patient. But the preliminary attempts are like watching a timorous bather who is frightened to dive into the water. Many testings of the temperature, many cautious extensions of the limbs, are necessary before the final plunge is taken.

This type of identification with parents is ultimately based upon the primitive morality of the super-ego, which is the morality of fear. "I must be the same as they are or they will be angry" is the operative phrase. "Good" is what parents approve of, and "bad" is what they dislike; and, naturally, they like themselves and their opinions. Most adults exhibit modes of behaviour which are not based upon reason or upon conscious choice, but upon parental attitudes which were introjected in childhood and which have never been discarded even though they may be inappropriate to present conditions. Super-ego standards are rigid, unrelated to the present, and emotionally defended. Reasoned argument makes but little impression upon opinions and modes of behaviour which cannot be altered without making the person concerned feel like a threatened child. We must all be familiar with people who are compelled to be perpetually busy; who cannot rest and who feel uncomfortable unless they are "doing something." Such people have taken into their psychic structure the notion that idleness is "bad" and activity is "good"; with the result that they will engage in any activity, however useless, rather than incur the inner reproach of laziness which torments them if they sit still.

Part of the process of self-realization consists, therefore, in discarding introjected beliefs and attitudes which prove to be foreign to the developing personality: and this may be attended by considerable anxiety and depression. In adolescence, for example, a new piece of self-discovery is often initiated by depression. Adolescents are notoriously moody, and often their fits of depression express their despair at finding that they are not "good" in the sense that they do not correspond to what they believe their parents expect of them, and are not just pocket editions of the parental models.

Becoming free of identification with others is never completed; and most of us remain to some extent prisoners of our family background, of our social class, or of our nationality. The club, the old boys' reunion, the perpetuation of hierarchical social structure, are mechanisms of reassurance. What a sense of solidarity, what an affirmation of mutual grandeur, is to be found at, for instance, a City dinner! The most platitudinous speech is acceptable in the alcoholic haze of good fellowship, and everything conspires to make us feel that we are all jolly good fellows (except, of course, for the waiters). The sense of mutual support which men gain from such gatherings is matched by the loss of their individual characteristics, and the subtleties of personality disappear in the simplicities of the crowd.

So far I have attempted to discuss identification from the negative point of view; but, as I pointed out at the beginning of this chapter, identification may also serve a positive function in the development of the personality. In searching for his own individuality the developing person may need to discard his identifications with those upon whom he has been dependent, and from whom he has feared to differ. He will also, however, tend to identify himself with people who appeal to him and who may play a valuable role in his development by evoking aspects of his personality which might otherwise lie latent.

CHAPTER 7

PROJECTION AND DISSOCIATION

Homo sum; humani nihil a me alienum puto.

TERENCE[1]

In the previous chapter we discussed the importance of ridding the personality of introjected attitudes and beliefs which did not belong to it, but which had been taken over wholesale from parents and other people upon whose goodwill the child depended. We must now consider the opposite process: that of recognizing and coming to terms with characteristics which have been denied and rejected in the course of development. Whereas introjection is the phenomenon in which characteristics belonging to others are attributed to oneself, projection is the phenomenon in which characteristics belonging to oneself are attributed to others. In the search for one's own individuality it is as important to recognize those parts of oneself which are projected upon others as to discard those parts of others which have been taken into oneself.

We have already postulated that the child, because of its dependence upon parental approval, strives to model itself upon those whom it has to please. This is a shift of the child's personality towards that of the parents, or towards what the child comes to believe that the parents are demanding of it. At the same time there will be a shift away from whatever seems to displease the parents; an attempt to deny and expel what they condemn, or what cannot be brought into the relationship with them. The child comes, therefore, to regard certain aspects of himself as dangerous or unpleasant, and so denies them. But these same characteristics, when he later meets them in other people, will disturb him; and he will tend to attribute to others, and to condemn in them, that which he cannot accept in himself.

The most extreme form of this type of projection is found in the paranoid psychoses, in which the patient believes himself to be the innocent victim of an unprovoked persecution. The delusional systems which paranoid patients exhibit are monotonously similar, since they are but variations upon the same basic themes; themes which stem from the sexual and aggressive impulses which the subject has been unable to accept himself, and which he therefore projects upon others. It is "they"—the others—who fill his mind with obscenities and excite peculiar sensations in his body, not he who has erotic feelings. It is "they" who are plotting to destroy him, not he who hates and shuns his fellow-men. It is "their" voices which whisper abuse in his ear at night, not his own thoughts and fantasies which torment him. That which is unacceptable is completely disowned, but found to be projected upon other people. The complete projection of the "bad" in such instances is a measure of the basic weakness and helplessness of the patient. It is only those who are emotionally extremely dependent who cannot afford to admit any of those characteristics which they believed as children to be regarded as "bad" by the parents, and which might, therefore, if admitted, threaten their security. The observation that those who later develop schizophrenia have often been unusually compliant, "good" children supports this conception. But in order to see this type of projection in action we need not examine the psychotic, nor even penetrate the psychotherapist's consulting-room; our daily experience will furnish a plenitude of examples.

Only a very moderate acquaintance with psychology is required to recognize that men constantly deplore in others that which they cannot accept in themselves, and that it is their own unadmitted inferiorities which excite their most violent condemnation. And so we find that it is generally the latent homosexual who fulminates against homosexuality, and the man who cannot come to terms with his own violent impulses who demands the revival of flogging. It is the woman who is unable to accept her own dependence and helplessness who cannot stand babies: and the denunciations of the militant atheist reveal how powerfully he has been affected by the religion against which he inveighs. A study of those people whom one most dislikes is a rewarding if painful task; for such a study reveals projected, and hence unadmitted, parts of one's own personality.

The peculiar bond which links together enemies has often been described. Two men who detest each other are closer emotionally than if they were politely detached, and ultimately more likely to make a relationship. This is an expression of the fact that hatred—like love—invariably contains a subjective element, and that there is something in common between two people who hate each other; for they hate that in themselves which the other appears to personify.

The principle that what we most condemn in others is some unadmitted part of ourselves is becoming generally accepted. Accepting a principle is, however, easy: but actually coming to terms with infantile aggression and sexuality which has been repressed is a painful and difficult process, attended by considerable fear and anxiety. To assimilate what is projected is as difficult as to discard what is introjected; and, in the psychotherapeutic endeavour, perhaps even more time will generally be spent in the former than in the latter process. Unadmitted parts of the personality generally display three characteristic features. They tend to be projected upon other people, they remain infantile, and they cause disturbance in the form of symptoms. Their projection upon others has been discussed above, but the other two features require further clarification.

It is a remarkable and interesting fact that parts of the personality which have been disowned in early childhood remain infantile; and even the experienced psychotherapist may sometimes be surprised by the appearance, in an apparently mature adult, of beliefs and attitudes appropriate to early childhood. It is as if a child coexisted with the adult personality—a child, moreover, whose earliest characteristics had been accurately preserved and who continued to feel and think in exactly the same way as in times long past.

Many estimable people are, for example, plagued with sexual fantasies and compulsions of an infantile, primitive kind which occasion them considerable distress and which are admitted to the psychotherapist only with the greatest difficulty. But if such fantasies are fully and honestly faced, if they are accepted to such an extent that they can be completely revealed to another person, their compulsive quality disappears, and the energy with which they are invested becomes available to the personality as a whole. That which cannot be fully admitted to another person is that which cannot be completely accepted by the individual himself; that which is unacceptable to the individual himself is inadmissible to another person. It is commonly believed that what can be admitted to oneself in the privacy of one's own solitude has been accepted: and that it is only material of which the individual is completely unconscious which it is hard for him to tolerate. But the difficulty which people experience in revealing disturbing fantasies, which may be fully conscious, indicates that there is in fact a vast difference between admitting something to oneself and actually telling someone else about it; and, as is implied in earlier chapters of this book, the maturing process, which includes the acceptance of the rejected, infantile parts of the personality, cannot take place in isolation. This is, I believe, the *raison d'être* of the psychotherapeutic process, which ultimately depends upon the relationship formed between patient and therapist.

That the unadmitted, rejected parts of the personality are those which cause symptoms is generally recognized; but, in the absence of some concept of self-realization, it is hard to see why this should be so. Freud gave us the valuable observations of "repetition-compulsion" and of the "return of the repressed"—and every psychotherapist must surely recognize that what has been rejected tends not only to persist and repeat itself in its infantile form, but also to demand recognition in the form of symptoms. Rejected parts of the personality are like children clamouring to be let into a room: they will continue to cause a disturbance until they are admitted. It is as if even the most infantile aspects of the personality, the aspects of which we should most like to rid ourselves, were endowed with a dynamic energy which demanded that they too should seek expression. Personality ultimately seeks realization as a whole, and, however much the ego may seek to reject that which it finds hard to tolerate, the rejected parts will make their appearance somewhere, whether as symptoms or as projections upon other people. The final aim is the realization of the total personality.

This chapter is headed "Projection and Dissociation" rather than "Projection and Repression" because I feel the need of a word which will express the rejection and splitting off of mental contents, but which does not necessarily imply that such contents are unconscious. Repression is, by definition, a process in which mental contents become unconscious; and what is repressed can only be disinterred by the use of one or other specialized techniques. There are, however, mental contents—thoughts, feelings, fantasies—which are felt to be alien to the personality, but which are not themselves deeply unconscious, although they may be masking other material which is. The sexual fantasies alluded to above come into such a category, and so do many obsessional thoughts. The term dissociation can include both such phenomena as these, and also the concept of repression, and I propose to use it as referring to all mental contents which are felt to be alien to the personality, whether conscious or unconscious.

Why is it that the mental contents which tend to be dissociated, and hence projected, chiefly consist of sexual and aggressive impulses? In the next chapter I hope to show that such contents are by no means the only ones to be projected, but it is in general true that the aspects of themselves which in this civilization people find hardest to confront are connected with sexuality and the drive for power. Jung,[2] in *The Undiscovered Self*, talks of "the world of unconscious instinct dominated by sexuality and the power drive (or self-assertion), corresponding to the twin moral concepts of Saint Augustine: *concupiscentia* and *superbia*.

The clash between these two fundamental instincts (preservation of the species and self-preservation) is the source of numerous conflicts."

The urge to power and the sexual instinct are also those aspects of the personality which cannot find expression in childhood and which necessitate conflict with the parents. So long as the parents are in power, so long is the child's assertion of itself incomplete: so long as the parents are its principal love-objects, so long is the expression of its sexuality impaired.

The hypothesis has been advanced in an earlier chapter that dependence and aggression are linked together: and, since every child is necessarily dependent, it follows that every child is inevitably aggressive. If the child is to establish itself as a separate personality, it is necessary that it should oppose itself to the parents, however tolerant and loving they may be—or else the child remains identified with the parents, a mere reflection of the parental psychology. Some parents seldom oppose their children at all. They give the children everything that they demand, are constantly at their beck and call, and subordinate their own personal lives completely to the wishes of the children. Such parents are depriving their children of anyone whom they can legitimately oppose, and by doing so are preventing their development. It is impossible to fight with someone who at once gives in; and so the child either becomes a tyrant or else becomes guilty about his perfectly normal aggressive feelings. A mother who is always self-sacrificing, who never asserts herself, and who has given up any claim to a life of her own is, by her example, likely to create the impression in her children that to oppose anyone else is wrong: and this may result in their disowning and trying to split off from their personalities those aggressive impulses which should play a valuable part in their development. The old-fashioned "progressive" school may be criticized on the same grounds. In a régime in which rebellion is impossible since everything is tolerated, there is less scope for individual development than in one in which teachers as well as pupils have their rights. Loving a child does not mean always giving in to it, but does imply accepting the fact that rebelliousness and opposition are a necessary and valuable part of growing up. Children need to fight with their parents, and for the parents to refuse ever to fight back is to treat the child as less than a person and to fail to maintain a relationship with it. One way, therefore, in which the child's aggressive feelings may become dissociated and partially denied is for it to be faced with a parent who always gives in: another is for it to confront a parent who never does so.

The tyrannical parent is perhaps less frequent than he was; and for many educated people the problem is rather that of exerting authority than that of tempering it. But it is clear that a child can be cowed by an excess of authority, and so terrified of its parents that it dare not oppose them. In such circumstances the child is equally unable to give expression to its aggressive feelings, and its development is also inhibited. Since any show of aggression on the part of the child results in punishment, it is natural that it should seek to deny feelings which arouse parental wrath and therefore induce insecurity. Aggression may thus be dissociated because a parent is too domineering or because he is too compliant: the ideal is to be found, as always, in the balance between two opposites. Since this balance is hard to attain, it is not surprising that, in many people, aggressive feelings have been subjected to dissociation and may give rise to neurotic symptoms. Indeed, the efforts of a considerable body of psychopathologists have for some time been directed much more to the understanding of aggressive impulses within the personality than to the study of sexuality.

It is easy to see how the child's aggressive impulses may become dissociated from its personality in the ways I have attempted to outline. Perhaps it is less easy to see how, in these days of enlightenment, sexuality may also come to be felt as partially alien. Since the concepts of psycho-analysis became part of the mental equipment of every educated adult, parents no longer condemn the manifestations of infantile sexuality in their children in the way in which Freud found that they did in *fin-de-siècle* Vienna. And yet sexuality and its offshoots remain a major and potent source of neurotic conflict; and such evidence as there is seems to indicate that children brought up in complete sexual freedom suffer the same difficulties at adolescence as their more conventionally reared contemporaries. It seems probable that some degree of guilt and anxiety about sexuality is inevitable: for, however tolerant the upbringing, it is generally impossible for sexual impulses to find full satisfaction within the home circle. So long as the child's behaviour is still predominantly under parental control, whether from without, by the actual parents, or from within, by the superego, so long will sexuality be to some extent a rejected part of the personality; for it is a part which cannot be expressed in actual behaviour, at least between parent and child, without the parent-child relationship being damaged.

It is worth considering why incest excites universal condemnation. It is not particularly uncommon, and most psychiatrists will have seen a number of examples. It is my impression that an incestuous relationship with a parent is usually harmful to a child, though incest with a brother or sister is not necessarily so. Indeed, sexual play with contemporaries, whether consanguineous or not, is so common that, in the absence of emotional difficulties with the parents, I cannot believe that it is itself productive of later difficulties. Incest between parent and child is objectionable firstly because, in a sexual situation, the parent abrogates parenthood. In our civilization a parent is required to be in command, to give security by being able to deal with circumstances and situations with which the child is not yet able to deal. If a parent is possessed by any violent emotion he is no longer a safe person, no longer a parent. Drunk parents, violent parents, frightened parents are also threats to a child's security, even if they are not amorous parents as well; for their loss of control makes them unable, at least temporarily, to fulfil the parental role.

Moreover, sex is apt to be terrifying where there is a marked discrepancy of power between the two people concerned; and most of us recoil from a situation in which intercourse is forced upon a weaker by a stronger person. Observation of the so-called "primal scene" is often interpreted by the child as frightening, for it frequently conceives the sexual act as an attack by the man on the woman. Since to the small child love means chiefly tenderness and protection, it is not surprising that adult passion is equated with violence, and that the incestuous advances of a parent are felt as a threat rather than as a manifestation of affection. In cases where the son or daughter is grown up this does not apply: and I have seen an example of an incestuous relationship between father and daughter which persisted for a considerable time. Eventually the father became intensely jealous of the daughter's feelings for another man and created such a disturbance that she reported him to the police, with the result that he was convicted and imprisoned. The continuance of such a relationship for months without undue disturbance on either side tends to demonstrate that it is not necessarily incest itself which is so damaging, but rather an emotional situation in which a child is exploited by an older and more powerful person. In incest between a parent and a young child the situation is bound to be one in which the child is not treated as a person, since it cannot participate in the situation on equal terms. It is thus being used rather than loved, treated as a thing, not an individual, and misused by the very person to whom it would normally turn for protection and security.

In adult life the complete expression of sexual love is only possible where each partner feels on equal terms with the other, where giving and taking is equal, and where each accepts the other as a whole person. This is why the psychoanalytic test of maturity, "genital primacy," is valid; although the terminology employed suggests a more limited concept than is actually implied. If one partner is markedly dependent upon the other, if, emotionally, one partner is a child and the other a parent, then the sexual relationship is bound to be unsatisfactory, for fear of the more powerful partner will impair the free expression of what either feels. When one partner is treated as a parent it is implied that one partner is weaker and the other stronger. A complete expression of sexual love requires that a man should be free of the fear that she will hurt him, and the same holds true of the woman also. The persistence of fears of this kind is usually related to the persistence of a childish sense of being less than the partner. This sense of inequality excites resentment on the one hand, and apprehension on the other: and so the ability to give and receive physical affection freely is impaired by the fear of physical hurt.

An adult patient whose father had made repeated incestuous advances to her in childhood was frightened of arousing any sexual feeling in a man, for to do so implied that he would hurt her. She projected the image of her father upon every man, felt that every man was powerful and that she was weak, and believed that any manifestation of affection towards her was bound to result in pain rather than in pleasure, since she felt like a helpless victim when confronted with a man, rather than like a woman who could play the feminine part on equal terms in a cooperative pleasure. She had to avoid evoking love from men because to do so meant that they would be cruel to her.

The sexual advances of a parent to a child need not necessarily be frightening; but there is a further, and perhaps even more important, objection to such incestuous relationships. Sexuality is, in adolescence, the main force which makes for independence. The adolescent is compelled by his increasingly urgent sexuality to seek relationships outside the home, since in the ordinary course of events there is but little scope for its expression within it. If sexuality can find free expression within the family circle there is so much the less reason for the child to leave it and strike out on its own, and persistent immaturity and dependence are the result.

A patient told me that his mother used to "act the part of a prostitute" towards him. His incestuous fantasies about her were perfectly conscious, and there was no evidence of the incest taboo in his material. But his immaturity was striking, and he was quite unable to act or take decisions in an adult or masculine way. He had never had to do so, and his reluctance to grow up was reinforced by the incestuous relationship with his mother, for, since he could gain a partial satisfaction with her, there was so much the less reason for his forming new and more adult relationships outside the home.

Incest between parent and child is, therefore, opposed to individuality, opposed to maturity, opposed to self-realization. By making sexuality either too easily accessible on the one hand, or too terrifying on the other, incest may encourage the persistence of immaturity or prevent the development of more adult attitudes. The deeply rooted distaste for incest which is attested by the legal penalties attached to it in our society can be shown to be based on rational as well as on emotional grounds; for incest can prevent or interfere with the growth and development of the individual, and, provided our basic hypothesis is accepted that the development of the individual to his fullest extent is desirable, it is easy to demonstrate that incest is to be deplored.

Since sexuality cannot be brought into the relationship between parent and child without disturbance of that relationship, it becomes evident that sexuality, like the aggressive impulses previously referred to, may become dissociated from the total personality and felt to be alien to it, even though the parents may have never explicitly condemned the early manifestations of it in their children or uttered the castration threats so often emphasized by the pioneers in psycho-analysis. The integration of sexuality, the full acceptance and recognition of its importance and the way in which it pervades every aspect of our being, is a valid test of maturity; for to realize sexuality in all its richness is to acknowledge separation from the parents and to act as an independent person. Parents often blame themselves unnecessarily for supposedly causing guilt and anxiety in their children. Of course they often do, and nobody supposes that a fiercely authoritarian upbringing, in which the child becomes cowed, is anything but harmful. But it is well to remember that the gradual emergence of the child as a separate individual is bound to be attended with some anxiety, and that this anxiety will be chiefly manifested in those aspects of the personality which we artificially dichotomize as sexuality and aggression, even though the upbringing of the child may have been as nearly ideal as can be imagined. It is therefore not surprising that, in adult life, those parts of himself which are denied by the subject, which tend to be projected, and which may give rise to symptoms, are intimately connected with the twin drives of power and sexuality which constitute the individual roots of his emergence as a separate individual.

CHAPTER 8

IDENTIFICATION AND PROJECTION

Now we have agreed that Love is in love with what he lacks and does not possess.   PLATO[1]

In a previous chapter an attempt was made to distinguish two types of identification. We pictured an infant who was at first quite unaware of his separate identity; and we postulated that the beginnings of personality development consisted in a gradual disidentification with the parents—the slow emergence from a matrix of a new and distinct person. We also concluded that this loss of primary identification was replaced by a secondary identification in which characteristics belonging to parents and others in authority were introjected for security reasons: and we were thus able to see that a child might come to exhibit traits which belonged not to itself but to those upon whom it was dependent. An introverted child brought up in a predominantly extraverted household, for instance, may appear to be much more in contact with other people than it actually is because it has assumed modes of behaviour which are foreign to its real personality.

Parents are bound to prove unsatisfactory objects of relationship for the developing child; and this is so for three reasons. First, since parents are in a position of authority, they are bound to be to some degree restrictive, and hence to excite resentment as well as affection. Second, a sexual relationship of a satisfactory kind with parents is impossible. Third, since no parents are perfectly endowed, they may lack qualities which would help to evoke potentialities in the child, which will be forced to turn to others instead of them to find what it needs. This third postulate requires expansion. It is difficult to imagine that Mozart could have been anything but a musician. But suppose that Leopold had been unmusical. Would Wolfgang's talent have matured so fast, would he have acquired at so early an age that mastery of technique which laid the foundation for his later achievement? A phenomenal endowment such as Mozart's will force its realization against considerable opposition; and the example of Handel attests the fact that even elderly and irascible physicians can be vanquished by their more gifted sons; but there can be little doubt that the realization of an innate potentiality in a child proceeds at a faster pace if his parents themselves exhibit something of the same gift or interest which is seeking expression.

During the course of development various people other than the parents, with whom the child comes in contact, may become emotionally important to it. The typical instance is the school-teacher. A favourite teacher may evoke latent potentialities in the child by providing a model with which the child can identify itself. Often such an identification goes temporarily too far and the child may, in its enthusiasm, take over attitudes and characteristics which again will be later discarded—just as in the case of the parents. But often something remains; some part of the child's personality has been evoked and continues to play its part in actual life.

Often the traits which are evoked in this way are those which the parents themselves do *not* exhibit, and which are therefore liable to remain latent unless the child comes across someone who will evoke them. This positive type of identification is an argument for the widest possible type of education; for the school with a wide range of staff, not the private tutor; for the university in which every variety of opinion is represented, not the specialized technical institution. For the varieties of temperament and the differences in hereditary endowment are extensive, and the more people with whom the child and adolescent can come in contact, the more quickly is he likely to find himself. It may be as well to emphasize here that this type of identification with school-teachers and others is not a conscious process of copying, but rests upon an emotional link between teacher and pupil which cannot be produced consciously. I am reminded here of a boy who, although intelligent, remained near the bottom of the class for a whole term. Next term he rose to a place near the top: and this was simply the result of a change of teacher. The boy was one who had failed to realize his potentialities partly because his father's attitude of anxious expectation had induced in him the conviction that nothing he did was worth while or ever likely to be. He was much in need, therefore, of a man who would give him what his father had been unable to provide; a feeling that his efforts were worth while and that he was capable of some achievement. Whereas the first teacher failed to convey this to the boy, the second succeeded; and this was reflected in the boy's change of position in the class. This is the kind of situation which leads to a partial identification of pupil with teacher. Because the pupil feels that the teacher approves of him, he reacts by taking over some of the teacher's characteristics. But this process does not occur with anyone: it occurs in response to a subjective need which the teacher happens to fulfil at that particular moment. In such a situation it is likely that, temporarily, the teacher will be seen as wholly "good" by the pupil, and that his attitudes and opinions will be taken over wholesale. Time will modify this, and further experience will reveal how much of what has been taken over really belongs to the pupil's own personality.

The type of identification described above is often, if not invariably, preceded by projection. We have already discussed the familiar type of projection in which characteristics which we cannot accept in ourselves are attributed to others. It is not, however, so generally recognized that more positive qualities are often projected also, and that this phenomenon is an important part of development.

The developing child is often *fascinated* by certain people; that is, these people have a strongly emotional effect upon him. It is natural enough that people should be attracted by those who resemble themselves and whom they recognize to be like themselves. It has been pointed out in the previous chapter that we like to have to do with people with whom we can identify—for it gives us a sense of solidarity and security in the world to find others who resemble us. But the compulsive attraction which rests upon the mechanism of projection is far more powerful than the link between those with whom it is easy to identify; and this is attested by the type of language which is generally used to describe it.

The phenomenon I mean is commonly referred to in the language of magic; and, although the words used have lost their compelling power through the abuse of habit, one can still detect in them the awe of the irrational which lurks in all of us. When we refer to a person as "fascinating," "bewitching," "enchanting," we may recognize that we are using terms originally appropriate to witchcraft and wizardry. A beautiful woman is "glamorous"; an orator "casts his spell" over us—we are at once in a realm where we recognize that their effect upon us is based upon something more powerful than reason.

In the course of development children are usually emotionally attracted to a whole series of people of both sexes. Such people are commonly school-teachers and older children; since these are the people outside the home with whom the child has most to do. The glamorization and idealization of such people is so much a part of normal development that it is taken for granted; but there can be few parents who have not sometimes been surprised by the intensity of feeling aroused in the breast of their child by some apparently dull and undistinguished person.

I believe that it can generally be shown that these people epitomize undeveloped parts of the child's own personality, and that they attract him so strongly because they stir a subjective response. It seems probably that those parts of the personality which are latent, undeveloped—and only potential, those parts, therefore, which can be said to be *unconscious*—are in fact *recognized* by the individual concerned, but, to start with, are thought to belong to others rather than to himself. Personality is like a harp with many strings. Not all the strings are plucked at once, and some may lie silent throughout life. Others may be set into vibration by the impact of personalities with the same frequency. The irrational attraction and sometimes adoration which an older child or a teacher will inspire in a pupil may be explained in terms of a projection of the latter upon the former. The child can be said, as it were, to "fall in love" with its own latent potentialities.

The psychological phenomenon of the "crush" or "passion" is often undervalued, and the explanations of it which are usually advanced seem to me inadequate. One such is that the child is simply looking for a substitute parent; another that this is merely a manifestation of the homosexual phase through which everyone passes (for such attractions are usually towards members of the same sex). I believe that these attractions are of great importance in psychological development, and that it is through such emotional attachments that the child discovers his own personality and becomes more aware of both his abilities and his limitations.

To the small child every adult is invested with a certain glamour simply because the adult can do things which the child cannot. The very attribute of being "grown up" is itself an attraction and something which every small child longs to exhibit in its own person. But the attractions with which I am here concerned are both more powerful and more specific than this. How often, for instance, will a latent capacity for appreciation or performance in the arts or in music be awakened in a child by a teacher whom the child admires. The emotional attachment which the child exhibits is a projection upon the teacher of the child's own capacity which, until the teacher evoked it, may have been latent and unrecognized. When this kind of projection occurs, there are two courses open to the child. The normal and desirable development is that the child should proceed from the stage of projecting upon the adult to that of identifying with him, and thus begin to model himself upon the teacher. As the child himself becomes capable of what hitherto has been thought to belong only to the teacher and not to himself, the emotional fervour of the attachment will die down. We only become emotionally involved with those who have got "something for us"; and when we ourselves have got it they no longer attract us to the same degree. A child "grows out" of someone to whom he was attracted because he has been able to develop in himself that which was originally projected upon the other. Even in adult life we all tend to overvalue skills which we do not ourselves possess; but we also no longer admire in others that which we can easily do ourselves.

The second and less desirable course is for the child to rest in the attitude of adoration in which he feels that the teacher continues to be wonderful but that he himself is incapable of reaching such heights. In such a case identification does not take place and the projection is not withdrawn. This persistence of projection without identification is an important feature of homosexuality.

Children in adolescence and during the years immediately preceding adolescence commonly idealize members of their own sex. The fact that this initial type of falling in love is generally homosexual is often attributed to segregation or to other environmental factors; but, in my view, it is a natural phenomenon which plays a positive and important part in emotional development. Whereas small children, though passionately interested in the differences between the sexes, do not usually split up into male and female groups, it is characteristic of older groups that they denigrate the opposite sex while exalting their own. The small child simply wants to "grow up," to gain some of the power which adults possess. In later childhood the boy is striving to be a man, and the girl to be a woman; and they tend to be fascinated by those people who possess qualities of masculinity and femininity which are as yet only latent in themselves.

The over-valuation of one's own sex combined with the under-valuation of the other is, perhaps, a necessary part of development; and in the initiation rites of primitive societies, in which youths pass from boyhood to manhood, it is usual for women to be rigorously excluded.[2] The seclusion of girls at puberty, though chiefly practised to avert the supposedly evil effects of their menstruation, may also be adduced as an example of the segregation of the sexes being thought desirable at certain stages of development.

E. M. Forster,[3] in his essay on "Jew-consciousness," describes how in his first preparatory school it was considered shameful to have a sister.

> Naturally anyone who had a sister hid her as far as possible, and forbade her to sit with him at a prize-giving or to speak to him except in passing and in a very formal manner.

At his second school,

> Sisters were negligible, but it was a disgrace to have a mother. Many tried to divert suspicion by being aggressive and foisting female parents upon the weak. One or two, who were good at games and had a large popularity-surplus, took up a really heroic line, acknowledged their mother brazenly and would even be seen walking with her across the playing field, like King Carol with Madame Lupescu.

Although concepts of masculinity and femininity vary widely from era to era and from place to place, it may be firmly asserted that there has been no era, and that there is no place, in which such concepts do not exist; and that it is a vital part of every child's development that it should become firmly established emotionally as a member of whichever sex it belongs to anatomically, and feel able to compete with other members of the same sex on equal terms.

It is generally accepted that an emotional interest which is predominantly directed towards members of the same sex is characteristic of childhood and the period up to the beginning of adolescence; and that, in many instances, this homosexual interest may persist until early adult life without there being anything abnormal or unusual about it. Homosexuality in the sense of a fixed adult pattern of behaviour cannot be said to exist until the middle twenties; for often the pattern spontaneously alters and the person becomes heterosexual long after the legal age of maturity has been attained. But many men and women remain predominantly interested in their own sex in exactly the same way as we accept as being natural at an earlier age. This is not simply a matter of the misdirection of the genital impulse, but of falling in love with a person, or at least with an idealized aspect of a person. Whether or not this falling in love is accompanied by a conscious wish for genital contact with the desired person seems to depend on age and on previous experience. Children habitually adore members of their own sex without wishing for genital contact because the genitals have not yet become the most important channel for the expression of their loving impulses. Adolescents and young adults may be more aware of the physical aspect of their desire, but homosexual fantasy is often only vaguely concerned with physical contact unless physical seduction has already occurred. There is a wish to be with the beloved person; to be noticed by him (or her); to talk of him; and a compulsive interest in all that he does; but the desire for physical union usually follows, rather than accompanies, the fascination which the beloved person exerts and, in the ordinary course of development, may never be made manifest at all.

Clinical experience of both male and female homosexual patients has convinced me that the most important psychological fact about confirmed homosexuals is their inner conviction that they can never be adequate members of their own sex who can compete with others on equal terms. For them it is always "the other man" who possesses masculinity, or "the other woman" who has feminine charm. Homosexuals are fascinated by that in others which they believe to be lacking in themselves—and, in the normal course of development, this fascination disappears because most people succeed in identifying themselves with adult members of their own sex. If you, a man, feel yourself to be a man among men, you will no longer accord to men that degree of admiration and esteem which you gave them when you were a boy. If you, a woman, feel yourself to be an attractive and poised member of your own sex, you will no longer be fascinated by the charms of those women upon whom you had "crushes" when you were growing up.

The persistence of a predominantly homosexual inclination indicates a failure of maturation—but a failure of a special kind—a failure to identify with adult members of the same sex, and a persistence of the projection upon them of those qualities of male and female maturity which, in the child and in the adult homosexual, are no more than latent.

The psycho-analytic view is that homosexual men (and other perverts) suffer from an intensification of the fear of castration which is a universal complex. My own observation leads me to suppose that it is not so much the fear of castration as the conviction of being castrated which is chiefly operative. Homosexual men are usually fascinated by the penis—both by their own organ, which they often regard as too small, and by that belonging to others, which they admire as being larger. It has been observed over and over again that men who are uncertain of themselves as men have a conviction that they have a small penis, and that other men are more generously endowed. This belief has, as a rule, nothing to do with reality. It is an outward, concretistic expression of an inner emotional conviction of being lacking in masculinity and unable to compete with other men on equal terms. The fascination which the male organ exerts compels homosexuals to look for it; and the compulsion to go into public lavatories in order to gaze at, or to touch, the genitals of other men is a symptom which is distressing to some homosexuals and not infrequently leads them to seek treatment. The larger the penis, the more does it excite their interest—an interest which is part of a wider and more general interest in "masculinity."

Homosexual men may themselves be effeminate, but they do not generally admire effeminacy in others. On the contrary, they are attracted by a rather extreme type of masculinity; and the over-muscular, tough young men who appear on the outside of physical culture magazines are the pin-ups of the homosexual male. They are drawn to just those qualities which they feel to be lacking in themselves, qualities which may in fact be latent rather than absent.

Proust,[4] in the famous essay on homosexuality which opens *Cities of the Plain*, describes homosexual men as

> lovers from whom is always precluded the possi-
> bility of that love the hope of which gives them
> the strength to endure so many risks and so much
> loneliness, since they fall in love with precisely that
> type of man who has nothing feminine about him,

who is not an invert and consequently cannot love them in return, with the result that their desire would be for ever insatiable did not their money procure for them real men, and their imagination end by making them take for real men the inverts to whom they had prostituted themselves.

Proust conceived of homosexual men as being psychologically feminine. In describing Charlus he says:[5]

He belonged to that race of beings, less paradoxical than they appear, whose ideal is manly simply because their temperament is feminine and who in their life resemble in their appearance only the rest of men; that where each of us carries, inscribed in those eyes through which he beholds everything in the universe, a human outline engraved on the surface of the pupil, for them it is that not of a nymph but of a youth.

We may sympathize with Proust's view and envy his insight, his observation, and his superbly subtle awareness of the motives of men and women: but we must disagree with his idea that the homosexual man is feminine. Rather is he a child whose development is incomplete—a boy who has not yet matured into a man. The homosexual search is often determined by an absence of a satisfactory identification in early life with the parent of the same sex; and in homosexual men it is common to find that the patient's father has been absent or in some way impossible to identify with. A father who is hard, unapproachable, and overbearing may inspire such fear that the developing boy turns away from him. A weak, soft, and ineffective father does not provide a sufficiently forceful personality to evoke masculine qualities in his son. In either case there is a failure of identification, and the son turns away from his father to seek in others those masculine attributes which he needs for his own development.

If all goes well he finds them and, by modelling himself upon a teacher or friend, himself becomes what he has been looking for in others. But, if he is sufficiently discouraged or frightened, he may continue to feel that other men possess something to which he can never aspire, and so remain in a state of immaturity.

A paradoxical effect of the failure of identification with one's own sex is the attempt to identify with the opposite sex: and the tweeds and flat heels, the assumed dominance of manner of the homosexual woman, conceal a deep hurt and feeling of inadequacy. In homosexual men the fear of women is usually strong enough to forbid identification with them; but transvestists, who are, as it were, half-way between homosexuality and heterosexuality, exhibit identification with the opposite sex in clear-cut form. Such men are usually deeply discouraged with themselves as men and feel they cannot possibly compete with others. But a lingering desire to shine, a normal wish to be recognized as *somebody*, finds expression in the fantasy that, if only they could be female, then they would be acceptable and even admired. In such cases of transvestism as I have seen and treated there has been no wish for sexual contact with men, but an envy of women, a wish to give up the struggle of trying to be a man and a desire to be a woman instead.

Similarly, a woman who has felt herself to be a failure as a member of her own sex often feels that life is so much easier for men; that if only she had been born a man her problems would be solved; and that it is an unfortunate accident that she is endowed with a female body when her soul is that of a man.

The process of becoming an adult member of one's own sex emotionally as well as physically serves as a striking illustration of how both projection and identification play their part in the development of the personality. That which is originally unconscious is at first conceived of as belonging to others, then assimilated as part of the person's own personality; and it is through contact with other personalities that the individual finds and identifies his own.

CHAPTER 9

HETEROSEXUAL LOVE
AND RELATIONSHIP

I attempt from love's sickness to fly in vain
Since I am myself my own fever and pain.

DRYDEN AND HOWARD[1]

In the last chapter the hypothesis was advanced that the compulsive attractions felt by the developing child towards members of its own sex were based upon projection, and that what was projected was an undeveloped part of the child's own personality. It was further suggested that, when a sufficient degree of maturity has been attained for identification with adult members of the same sex to take place, the projections upon them are withdrawn and emotional interest shifts to the opposite sex. To be able to fall in love with the opposite sex implies a more or less firm identification with one's own, and also an identification with being "grown up," although, as with all psychological processes, outlines are never sharp and stages never completed. There are obviously many people who seek a parent in their heterosexual partner; but such people can hardly be said to be falling in love in the full sense, and a study of their psychology invariably reveals the presence of sexual fantasies which have little or nothing to do with the partner, but which contain those aspects of sexuality which they feel to be incompatible with the real person. A woman who has married a kind and gentle elderly man, to whom she is really a daughter, will tend to have fantasies of a ruthless and powerful young lover who is perpetually engaged in abducting her to some romantic destination. A man whose woman is a mother to him will be preoccupied with day-dreams of an invariably seductive courtesan whose sole *raison d' être* is to inflame his sensuality. The more paternal or maternal the partner, the more insistent will be the fantasies: and a study of the conscious relationship enables one to predict the type of day-dream with some confidence.

In addition to this type of parent-child relationship between the sexes, all kinds of stages of intermediate between homo- and heterosexuality can be observed: and a study of the fantasies of those people in whom heterosexuality is as yet not firmly established is of considerable interest. If such material could be adequately codified it would provide us with objective evidence of the process of sexual development; for it is not generally realized (except by purveyors of pornographic literature) that these fantasies are far more collective than individual and, as such, give a picture of the general development of the sexual instinct in man rather than in a particular person.

For instance, some male homosexuals who are still predominantly fascinated by the male may yet admit to fantasies in which their favourite man is observed to be having intercourse with a woman. Sometimes the subject himself is watching the procedure with interest; sometimes he then, or concurrently, has relations with the man: and frequently he follows the man in having intercourse with the woman. Uncertain himself of how to deal with her, and feeling his own instinct to be an inadequate guide, he requires a lead from the man whom he so much admires, and whom he can only then attempt to emulate.

Of a similar kind are the fantasies in which a wife has to be brought to heel by another man before she will be sufficiently compliant to submit to her husband. Elaborate sadistic fantasies in which, for example, the woman is sent to a school for wives in which she is beaten into submission by a stern schoolmaster, are not uncommon, and form the stock in trade of pornographers whose function is to provide solace for those who are not yet able to find love in a more orthodox manner. Nor are such fantasies confined to the pages of vulgar magazines. Several writers of thrillers, whose work is acclaimed by the critics and public, have produced books which are little more than a series of such fantasies interspersed with padding designed to give the appearance of coherent stories. The catalogue of these phenomena has yet to be compiled in such a way as to illustrate the thesis which I am advancing; that such fantasies are not merely distasteful aberrations, but also compensatory strivings towards normality, which may be hesitant stages on the path of development, as in the examples given above. They are mentioned here simply to illustrate the fact that there are many intermediate steps on the way to sexual maturity. There may be no clearly defined moment at which the boy realizes that, for him, magic is no longer to be found in the toughness of the male, but rather in the softness and delicacy of her whom he so lately despised: and it might be hard for the girl to remember when first her heart beat faster at the sight of the boy whom yesterday she dismissed as rough and noisy.

In the last chapter we noted that those compulsive attractions which are based upon projection are referred to in the language of magic; and we assumed that this magical quality was due to the projection of a subjective element— an undeveloped part of the personality. This conception is,

I believe, valuable in helping us to understand and appreciate the homosexual infatuations of young people. Does it also apply to heterosexual falling in love?

In the *Symposium*[2] the idea that men fall in love with, or are fascinated by, what seems to be lacking in themselves is advanced by Socrates in characteristic fashion:

> "Is the nature of Love such that he must be love of something, or can he exist absolutely without an object? I don't mean 'Is love love of a particular mother or father?'—to ask whether Love is love of a mother or father would be absurd—but I can make my point clear by analogy. If I were to take the single notion *Father* and ask 'Does *Father* mean the father of someone or not?' you, if you wanted to give the right answer, would presumably reply that *Father* means the father of a son or a daughter, wouldn't you?"
>
> "Certainly," said Agathon.
>
> "And similarly with *Mother*?"
>
> "Agreed."
>
> "Let us go a little further, to make my meaning quite clear. The notion *Brother*, does that intrinsically imply brother of someone, or not?"
>
> "Of course it does."
>
> "In fact, of a brother or sister?"
>
> "Yes."
>
> "Very well. Now try to tell me whether Love means love of something, or whether there can be Love which is love of nothing."
>
> "Quite clearly, it means love of something."
>
> "Take a firm grasp of this point then," said Socrates, "remembering also, though you may keep

it to yourself for the moment, what it is that Love is love of. And now just tell me this: Does Love desire the thing that he is love of, or not?"

"Of course he does."

"And does he desire and love the thing that he desires and loves when he is in possession of it or when he is not?"

"Probably when he is not."

"If you reflect for a moment, you will see that it isn't merely probable but absolutely certain that one desires what one lacks, or rather that one does not desire what one does not lack. To me at any rate, Agathon, it seems as certain as anything can be. What do you think?"

"Yes, I think it is."

"Good. Now would anybody wish to be big who was big, or strong who was strong?"

"It follows from my previous admission that this is impossible."

"Because a man who possesses a quality cannot be in need of it?"

"Yes."

"Suppose a man wanted to be strong who was strong or swift-footed who was swift-footed. I labour the point in order to avoid any possibility of mistake, for one might perhaps suppose in these and all similar cases that people who are of a certain character or who possess certain qualities also desire qualities which they possess. But if you consider the matter, Agathon, you will see that these people must inevitably possess these qualities at the present moment, whether they like it or not, and no one presumably would desire what is inevitable. No, if a man says: 'I, who am healthy, or am rich, none-theless desire to be healthy or rich, as the case may be, and I desire the very qualities which I possess,' we should reply: 'My friend, what you, who are in possession of health and wealth and strength, really wish, is to have the possession of these qualities continued to you in the future, since at the present moment you possess them whether you wish it or not.' Consider, then, whether when you say 'I desire what I possess' you do not really mean 'I wish that I may continue to possess in the future the things which I possess now.' If it were put to him like this, he would agree, I think."

"Yes," said Agathon.

"But this is to be in love with a thing which is not yet in one's power or possession, namely the continuance and preservation of one's present blessings in the future."

"Certainly."

"Such a man, then, and everyone else who feels desire, desires what is not in his present power or possession, and desire and love have for their object things or qualities which a man does not at present possess but which he lacks."

"Yes."

"Come then," said Socrates, "let us sum up the points on which we have reached agreement. Are they not first that Love exists only in relation to some object, and second that that object must be something of which he is at present in want?"

Like poor Agathon, we can only answer "Yes" to this remorseless argument: but, if our hypothesis that compulsive attractions are based upon projection is to stand, we need to add something to the statement of Socrates. We have already suggested that the compulsive, magical quality which is the characteristic feature of the state of being in love, is due to the projection of a subjective element. The Greeks were well aware of this, and, in an even better-known passage in the *Symposium*, Aristophanes puts forward an explanation.

He recalls the myth that there were originally three sexes—hermaphrodite, male, and female. When Zeus, incensed by the hubris of these creatures, decided to sever them in half, each sex was left incomplete and was compelled, therefore, to seek out a partner who would make it whole once more. Thus the male sought a male, the female a female, and the bisected hermaphrodite its contrasexual partner. "Love," says Aristophranes, "is simply the name for the desire and pursuit of the whole."

The Greeks of the fifth century B.C. evidently felt the same need as ourselves for an explanation of the compulsive and magical quality of Love, and recognized the subjective element which they personified as the lost half of the bisected whole. In finding a lover a man was therefore discovering the other side of himself, and the same was true for a woman. Recognizing and accepting homosexuality as they did, the Greeks found it necessary to postulate three different original types of people: whereas we regard both male and female homosexuality as precursive stages to heterosexuality, although realizing that many people are unable to pass beyond the homosexual phase of development. The high value which the Greeks attributed to masculinity, and the comparatively lowly position of women in their society, perhaps explains why male homosexual love was valued above the love of women. Our values are different and we regard homosexual love as inferior and condemn it when it is prolonged into adult life. But we can entirely agree with the conception of the desire and pursuit of the whole, and with the idea that people in love are seeking not only for sexual satisfaction but for the other half of themselves.

It seems that no sooner have adolescents reached the stage of identifying with their own sex in a more or less adult fashion than they begin to be fascinated by that which they appear to lack—the attributes of the opposite sex. That heterosexual falling in love is based upon projection is universally accepted, although the technical term may not be used. We all know that the beloved as regarded by the lover is not identical with the person seen by everyone else: and that falling in love involves an over-valuation, and a distorted picture, of the person who is loved. To us a girl may seem ordinary: to him she "walks in beauty like the night." To us a man appears commonplace: to her he is a romantic hero. It is inevitable that beauty is predominantly in the eye of the beholder, and that the image of the beloved is an expression of a subjective need rather than a picture of an actual person. But what is this subjective need and from where does the contrasexual image originate?

It is obvious that the sexual instinct itself seeks fulfilment, and that its frustration or lack of object will give rise to an imaginary object: so that men without women, and women without men will, inevitably, like St. Antony, be surrounded by a host of incubi and succubi who take possession of their imagination and personify the object which is missing. But to be in love is an experience which to my mind is inadequately explained in terms only of the need for genital satisfaction; for this may be and often is attained without two people being in love with each other. If we are to be consistent in assuming that the irrational, magical quality associated with falling in love is always due to the projection of a subjective element, then we cannot escape the hypothesis that we are all in some sense bisexual—or, rather, that all those who become capable of falling in love with the opposite sex are so constituted, for it is clear that no experience is more magical than falling in love; and it is also apparent that no experience is more manifestly subjective. In his state of infatuation the lover seems to conceive of union with the beloved as the be-all and end-all of existence. Lovers feel as if they were made for each other; as if no one else could possibly fulfil their need; as if no one could conceivably be as fortunate as themselves; as if they themselves were *incomplete* without the other person. The projection of the subjective element is obvious.

In this connexion it is interesting to note that, at the outbreak of a schizophrenic psychosis, the patient frequently believes that a change of sex is taking place. I have suggested that identification with one's own sex is an important part of development: and it is clear that it is the conscious part of the personality, the ego, which is identified in this way. In acute schizophrenia the ego is no longer in command; it is, as it were, swamped by the unconscious, and the patient is at the mercy, rather than in control, of his emotions. The patient not infrequently expresses his fear of being overwhelmed in this way as a fear of change of sex; as if the ego was identified with the anatomical, actual, sex of the patient, and the unconscious with the opposite sex.

The anatomical abnormality of hermaphroditism is so rare as to be a medical curiosity. But occasionally a hermaphrodite will elect, or be encouraged, to "change sex"; that is, to adopt the manners and behaviour of the sex opposite to that in which he or she had up to date been reared. Such an occurrence excites an outburst of publicity of such proportions as to suggest that the emotional interest in change of sex is a collective rather than an individual phenomenon, and tends to attest the fundamental bisexuality of human beings.

The mutual projection which occurs between lovers seems to indicate a search for completeness, a reaching out after wholeness, a union between conscious and unconscious: so that, to the man, the woman appears to contain all that is missing in himself and all that would complete his life; and, while a fundamental part of what is missing is a partner with whom he can have intercourse, this is not the only need which she promises to fulfil. For him she personifies whatever, in his particular culture, is called feminine; and for her he is the embodiment of masculinity. The image which each projects upon the other exhibits the psychological, as well as the anatomical, attributes which distinguish the sexes; and the fact that the psychological attributes vary from time to time and from place to place does not invalidate this concept. The Mundugumor[3] may differ from the Arapesh in their ideas of what is masculine and what is feminine; yet the fact that the sexes are distinguished by more than their anatomy is common to every civilization. The forms in which masculinity and femininity manifest themselves may vary; the fact that there are such manifestations remains the same.

The scheme of development propounded by the older type of psycho-analysis ends, like the Victorian novel, with a happy marriage—or, to use jargon, with the attainment of genital primacy: and, in earlier Freudian writings, one might be forgiven for assuming that the achievement of satisfactory heterosexual intercourse was the final aim of human relationship.

Of course, the fascination which each sex exerts upon the other leads to heterosexual relationships, and to the establishment of the genital, as the main channel for the giving and receiving of love: but, if our view is correct, the achievement of genital primacy and the becoming an adult member of one's own sex is not the whole of development. A further stage exists in which the heterosexual projection is withdrawn, in the same way as in the homosexual phase; a stage of development in which being "in love" is superseded by loving, in which projection is replaced by relationship.

This is not to deny the continuing need of each sex for the other; anatomy alone demands that this be recognized. But the absence of compulsion—the withdrawal of projection—must be recognized as a stage of development beyond that in which the individual is at the mercy of such feelings. However delightful it is to be in love—and, in retrospect, the torments which accompany the delights are apt to be forgotten—it is still an advance to be able to love without the distortion of the other person which the projection of the contrasexual image necessarily involves. Were a man to be marooned on a desert island with one female companion it is probable that his subjective need would invest her with a glamour which she would not appear to possess under more normal circumstances: it is only when we no longer compulsively need someone that we can have a real relationship with them. None of us is ever completely whole; nor can our need of each other, and therefore our distortion of each other, be entirely dispelled; but, if we are sufficiently fortunate in our partner, and if our relationship is a progressive thing, not merely a static achievement, we may approximate to a stage in which, because each fulfils the other's need, each is also treated as a whole person by the other. Whereas formerly two people in love served only to complete what each felt to be lacking—now two whole people confront each other as individuals.

The attainment of this stage of development is marked also by a diminution of the competitive striving so characteristic of young people who are not yet certain of themselves as men or women. Much psychotherapeutic time is habitually spent in exploring such uncertainties, and in trying to reduce the compulsive struggles in which men feel forced to prove themselves stronger than other men; in which women have to show that they are better than other women. To the adolescent the world is peopled with impossibly masculine men, and inconceivably feminine women, none of whom could ever be emulated by an actual human being. But, with the attainment of a real relationship with the opposite sex, the need for such vehement affirmation of one's own sex disappears; and the possibility of a real relationship with oneself emerges—that self which is neither all male nor all female, but a mixture of both.

A happy marriage perhaps represents the ideal of human relationship—a setting in which each partner, while acknowledging the need of the other, feels free to be what he or she by nature is: a relationship in which instinct as well as intellect can find expression; in which giving and taking are equal; in which each accepts the other, and I confronts Thou.

CHAPTER 10

THE PSYCHOTHERAPEUTIC PROCESS

*Only connect the prose and the passion, and both will
be exalted, and human love will be seen at its height.
Live in fragments no longer. Only connect and the beast
and the monk, robbed of the isolation that is life to
either, will die.*　　　　　　　　　　E. M. FORSTER[1]

This book began with the observation that the results of
psychotherapy did not seem to depend upon the school to
which the psychotherapist belonged, nor upon the method
which he employed (although there is an important reservation with regard to method to which I shall refer later).
There have in fact been investigations into psychoanalytic
technique which show that, even within the same school,
therapists differ widely in what they do. They vary not only
in the beliefs which they hold, but in innumerable lesser
ways which may, nevertheless, be of importance; as, for
example, in how often the patient is seen, in whether he
lies on a couch or sits up, in the timing of interpretations,
and in the degree of activity of the therapist. However valuable schemes of technique may be, there is no doubt that,
in practice, there are all kinds of variations in how therapists actually behave; and that, since investigation within
the comparatively formalized school of psychoanalysis has
shown such variability, investigation into the practice of
other, less formalized, psychotherapeutic schools would
show an even greater range of individual differences. This

being so, it is hard to defend the proposition that the results of psychotherapy depend upon the technique employed.

It can, of course, be argued that there are no results of psychotherapy, and that the recovery of some patients who have been treated by psychotherapy is fortuitous. The fact that neurotic symptoms vary in severity, and that a good many people appear to lose their symptoms spontaneously has been adduced as evidence that psychotherapy is unnecessary, and that as many people recover without, as with, its aid. It is significant that the most virulent attack upon psychotherapy in recent years has come from a professor of psychology who has no medical qualification and who has never been responsible for the clinical care of patients; and, while we may accept his strictures upon the lack of scientific evidence as to the results of psychotherapy, we may justifiably suspect the opinions of one who has no experience in the treatment of neurosis, and who has never felt obliged to try and help a fellow human being in distress of mind, even though there is as yet no absolute proof that such help is effective.

I am inevitably prejudiced in favour of psychotherapy, and I believe that it is effective in a large proportion of cases of neurosis and in some psychotic cases also. But, even if it could be proven that psychotherapy was not effective (and that is as hard to do as to prove that it is) we should still, as patients, and still more as human beings, be called upon to make some attempt to care for people in distress of mind: and this would inevitably result in our trying to make some relationship with such people. We should, therefore, be driven into psychotherapy even if we disbelieved in its efficacy: for, as I see it, psychotherapy consists fundamentally in two people attempting to make a relationship with each other. The view of human development which I have outlined is based upon a fundamental hypothesis derived from the practice of psychotherapy: this is, that the development of personality and the development of object-relationships are ultimately aspects of the same process, and that to talk of personality as if it existed apart from interpersonal relationships is meaningless.

In my search for an explanation of the efficacy of psychotherapy I am forced to the conclusion that the underlying common factor is the development of the relationship between the patient and the psychotherapist. Methods and theories differ widely: but every psychotherapeutic situation contains at least two people—a therapist and a patient—and, although in group psychotherapy the relationship formed between members of the group may be more important than that formed between therapist and patient, this does not contradict the hypothesis: for in group psychotherapy the other members of the group are acting as therapists *vis-à-vis* each other, since they provide for each other the possibility of new relationships in a special therapeutic setting—which is the characteristic feature of the situation in individual psychotherapy also.

At this point I feel obliged to state the reservation as to *method* in psychotherapy to which I referred at the beginning of this chapter. I believe that there is a considerable difference between psychotherapy in which persuasion, suggestion, and hypnosis are the principal methods employed, and psychotherapy which is predominantly analytic. Analysts of quite different training and fundamental beliefs will unite in regarding suggestion and hypnosis as inferior forms of treatment. Even if they admit that there is a place in psychotherapy for such methods they will agree that suggestion is in a way opposed to the aim of analysis. There is a very real divergence of practice and personality between those therapists who use an analytical approach and those who rely predominantly on suggestion; and this divergence rests upon a different fundamental aim. A simple example may serve to illustrate this. Suppose that a hypnotist suggests to a patient that he will become more independent, more able to make his own decisions, more confident. If the patient responds to these suggestions it may appear that a satisfactory result has been achieved. But it is justifiable to inquire upon what basis this new-found independence rests. If a man becomes more independent simply because another person tells him he ought to do so, it must be doubtful whether he really wants to be more independent, and even more doubtful whether his apparent independence will be sustained. The ability to do what one is told is not good evidence of a development towards maturity. It is the dominant position of the therapist and the correspondingly submissive position of the patient which makes suspect all techniques of psychotherapy based on suggestion; for to dominate another person is to treat him as less than a whole person and, ultimately, to interfere with his development towards being a whole person in his own right.

This is not to deny that suggestion plays a part in psychotherapy of an analytical type. It is bound to do so; and even the most detached, impersonal, and unemotional analyst cannot avoid influencing the patient by tone of voice, emphasis, and inflexion, and even by comparatively impersonal things such as the room in which the patient is seen.

But the attitude towards the patient of the therapist who deliberately uses hypnosis and suggestion is very different from that of the analyst, and is, I believe, less calculated to encourage the development of the individual. Jung states that men only react positively to those suggestions with which they are secretly in accord anyway: and so implies that the part played by suggestion in analytical psychotherapy is unimportant, although admitting that it occurs. But the difference in attitude of the analyst compared with that of the hypnotist is important. A method of treatment such as hypnosis, which rests upon the prestige of the doctor and which inevitably keeps the patient upon an inferior footing, may be of temporary service: but ultimately fails to encourage the separate development of the individual as a unique person, since it depends upon the patient accepting what the doctor suggests, which is bound to prevent him from forming a relationship with the doctor on equal terms.

The analytical approach, on the other hand, constantly demands of the patient that he should himself solve his own problems, and does not require that he should agree with the doctor or take over his ideas. The function of the analyst is to make clear what the problems are, not to provide ready-made solutions; and the avoidance of didacticism is designed to encourage the patient's independence.

Marcus Aurelius obtained for Commodus the best possible teachers; but the solicitousness of the most cultured served only to produce the most vicious of all the Roman Emperors. Lord Chesterfield subjected his son to the most intensive correspondence course in manners of which we have a record: but Stanhope remained obdurately unaffected and continued to prefer his library to the world of power and fashion in which his father was so anxious that he should posture successfully. Analysts do well to shun didactic types of psychotherapy, just as fathers are best advised to avoid trying to instruct their sons; for in either case the recipient of their well-intentioned but ill-considered teachings may rise up in wrath and say, "But who are you that you should tell me how to live?" And to this most pertinent question there is no adequate reply.

I have suggested above that the effectiveness of analytical psychotherapy depends upon the relationship formed between analyst and patient. This is, I believe, the common factor underlying the diverse beliefs and practices of the various analytical schools. This hypothesis can be further extended by postulating that the degree of recovery which takes place in the patient is proportional to the degree of maturity of the relationship which he is enabled to make with the therapist. If I am right in believing that neurotic symptoms are an expression not only of disharmony within the individual himself, but also of a failure in the maturation of his relationship with others; if in fact these are but two ways of looking at the same thing, then it must follow that the gradual resolution of neurotic symptoms is accompanied by an increasing maturity in the relationship between the patient and therapist which, in the most favourable instances, culminates in their confronting each other as whole human beings upon equal terms. No one is more aware than I am that such an outcome of psychotherapy is not always possible; but I like to know the direction in which I am aiming, even if many of my arrows fall short of the mark.

All psychological schools of an analytic kind, and some others which are not (for example, those concerned with learning theory) seem to agree that neurosis and psychosis are intimately related to disturbances in development. The Freudian school lays emphasis upon emotional disturbances in the early years of childhood; the Kleinians postulate difficulties in the first few weeks or months of life; and even Jung, who stresses the present disharmony of the psyche and the pointers to the future which may be implicit on the patient's material, states that neurosis is due to a one-sided development of personality which can be traced back to the slenderest beginnings in childhood.

In an earlier chapter we discussed the dissociation and rejection of those parts of the personality which were felt to be alien to the subject: and we concluded that these aspects of himself were rejected because the child had come to feel, rightly or wrongly, that they were incompatible with the parents; and that, because he was not yet ready to be independent of his parents, he was compelled to tailor his personality to fit in with their supposed requirements. In other words, it was postulated that a partial dissociation of the child's personality took place because he was either not accepted, or at any rate came to feel that he was not accepted, as a whole person, by the parents, and consequently could not accept himself as a whole person. One result of this (partially inevitable) failure of acceptance was that the child tended to identify himself with only that in himself of which the parents seemed to approve, and to reject that in himself of which the parents seemed to disapprove; and it was suggested that it was these rejected aspects of the personality, chiefly consisting of aggressive and sexual impulses, which gave rise to symptoms in later life.

The grosser degrees of dissociation of the personality can, I believe, only be healed by the development of a relationship with another person in which the patient comes to feel accepted more as a whole and can therefore come to accept himself more as a whole. At the beginning of the psychotherapeutic process the therapist is bound to be more or less in the position of a parent *vis-à-vis* the patient. The fact that neurosis is a kind of immaturity or childishness, as well as the fact that the patient is seeking help from the therapist, inevitably puts the latter in a position of authority; although it is a position from which he hopes to descend progressively during the course of treatment. It has already been suggested that a good parent is one who is able to give the child that loving acceptance which encourages its development and differentiation as a separate individual and which does not demand that it shall conform to a prearranged pattern. It is this same attitude which is required of the psychotherapist; the attitude which Jung describes as "unprejudiced objectivity." I do not believe that it matters to which school the therapist belongs, nor which beliefs or theories he holds, if he himself is capable of this attitude of objective love. If he has this attitude he is providing what is possibly the most important requirement for the patient in any form of psychotherapy—a milieu in which development can proceed. I have postulated that all men are seeking self-realization—the full flowering of the personality; and that such a flowering can only take place in the fruitful soil of satisfactory interpersonal relationships. It may be that it is the degree to which the therapeutist can provide this soil which determines his therapeutic success or failure.

If I am right in supposing that it is, above all, this milieu in which he feels accepted as a whole which the patient is seeking, it is pertinent to inquire why he needs a psychotherapist to provide it. There are a great many people in the world who are anxious to help others and who are prepared to spend time and trouble over their problems. Moreover, it is not uncommon that during the course of analytical psychotherapy the patient forms a relationship with someone other than the therapist who proves of as much or more help to him. Some therapists discourage such relationships on the ground that they interfere with the transference situation; but, as a general rule, any relationship which lessens the emotional isolation of the patient is to be welcomed provided that it is not also one in which he is liable to be swamped. Psychotherapists tend to feel uneasy about the help proffered to their patients by friends, not because they wish to keep the therapeutic situation a closed one, but because they fear that the friend may fall into the trap of trying to order the patient's life for him, rather than enabling him better to order his own. It is difficult enough for the therapist, trained as he should be by the analysis of his own personality, to avoid interfering with his patients: but it is much more difficult for friends. The reason for seeking help from a psychotherapist rather than from a friend is that the former is less likely to be subjectively involved with the patient, and therefore more likely to be able to provide what the patient needs. Moreover, the psychotherapist is often confronted with people whose friends have long ago given up trying to make any intimate relationship with them, since they have found it too difficult to do so. It is those who are most in need of human contact who find it impossible to procure it, since their fears of others preclude them from ever getting close to anyone; and their acquaintances are apt to desist from attempting intimacy with one who either rebuffs them or shrinks away. It is perhaps especially the very introverted, schizoid patients that the psychotherapist finds both most difficult and also most rewarding; for it is such people who demand his greatest skill. Simple cases of anxiety can often be helped by anyone who has the goodwill and time to give to them; but really isolated personalities demand an approach and an understanding which can be acquired only through specialized training.

The relationship with the therapist makes possible the

healing of the dissociation within the patient; the acceptance of the previously unacceptable, the integration of the formerly inadmissible. But, the inquirer may ask, there are surely such repulsive aspects of human nature, such horrors within all of us, that it is impossible to accept or integrate them. Many people are horrified by the grisly catalogue of psychopathological phenomena—the murderous, incestuous, and perverse fantasies which lurk in the back bedrooms of our minds. Analytical investigation may bring such things into consciousness; but while insight may illumine, it frequently fails to dispel these fantasies; and the intellectual appreciation of their infantile origins does not necessarily speed maturation. Is not the only possible course to admit and face the primitive in ourselves and then firmly to close the door and allow it no further expression?

If, however, the hypotheses which have so far been advanced are correct, it follows that the horrifying and primitive aspects of the psyche only remain horrifying and primitive if they are unrelated to the whole, and therefore unrelated to other people. The devil only remains devilish if he is dissociated from the deity from whom he took his origin. The aggressive fantasies which are so characteristic of early childhood and which, if they are still active in adult life, cause such distress to kindly characters who would in reality not harm a fly, remain in this primitive form because the person concerned has also remained childish, and has never been able to utilize the aggressive energy which would have become available to him if it had not been disowned at an early stage in his development.

There are many people who, for instance, suffer from obsessional thoughts of violence and who are frightened of seeing or reading about any manifestation of violence—a fear which greatly restricts the forms of entertainment available to them in our civilization. It can regularly be demonstrated that, in their daily relationships with each other, such people are too compliant, too yielding, too submissive. The aggressive energy which is locked up in their symptoms is actually energy which should be finding expression in life; and which would contribute to the achievement of a more adult attitude if it were allowed to do so. The more submissive the patient is in reality, the more aggressive will he be in dream and fantasy: the more he is able to make adult relationships on equal terms, the more will the infantile, pathological, and unacceptable aspects of his aggressiveness disappear. It is the attainment of a new kind of relationship with others and with himself which ultimately heals the patient; and, in the more severe dissociations of personality, this healing can only take place via the psychotherapist. The changing relationship with the therapist becomes a bridge which leads to the formation of more adult ties with people outside the therapeutic situation, and it is this changing relationship which constitutes the transference.

CHAPTER 11

TRANSFERENCE AND COUNTER-TRANSFERENCE

Opposition is true friendship.   WILLIAM BLAKE[1]

In spite of innumerable expositions the subject of transference remains controversial. There is probably no aspect of analytical psychotherapy which is regarded with more suspicion or with less understanding. The fact that transference is both spontaneous and inevitable; that it occurs outside as well as inside the therapeutic situation; that it cannot be engineered, and that it would not be desirable to induce it artificially even if it were possible to do so—all this is but little appreciated by the public, by doctors, and even by psychiatrists without analytical training. The popular belief that analysis involves falling in love with the analyst, and that therapeutic success depends upon this, dies hard; and, in the face of such a belief, it is not surprising that the analytical process is regarded with suspicion. For who would choose deliberately to enter a situation so fraught with danger, so apt for exploitation, and so potentially painful as falling in love with an unknown person who, by the nature of that same situation, is unable to reciprocate? It would be idle to deny that, in the course of analytical psychotherapy, powerful feelings of both love and hate do often, though not invariably, become focused upon

the therapist: but, if the nature of the transference phenomenon is fully apprehended, the fact of the emergence of
such feelings will be appreciated as a spontaneous and inevitable phenomenon, which springs from the subjective
state of the patient rather than from the machinations of
the therapist, who indeed would be thankful to be spared
the labour of dealing with such difficult manifestations.

That transference is a form of projection is generally
appreciated; and we owe to Freud the original and illumi-
nating concept of the projection of parental figures upon
the therapist. It is not surprising that the figures projected
in this way are, in the first instance, chiefly parental, although the image of any person who has been emotionally
important to the patient may also appear: for, as suggested
in the last chapter, the relationship between patient and
therapist is bound to be emotionally comparable to that
between child and parent, at least as regards the problems
for which the patient is seeking help. We are all children
when faced with difficulties which we do not understand,
and, although a patient may be adult and mature in many
respects, his emotional problems will disclose the child con-
cealed behind the adult exterior. Moreover, it is a truism
to state that our relationship to an unknown person is conditioned by the kind of relationships we have had in the
past. It is impossible for us to meet a new person, especially
one from whom we hope for help, without some degree of
prejudice derived from previous experience. It is common
to find out our opinion of a new acquaintance changes as
we get to know him better; and this change is not simply
the result of finding out more about him, but of correcting
the partially distorted picture of him which our imagination
had already constructed. Perhaps ideally we should approach a stranger without preconceptions; but, in practice,

our image of him is a complex one, compounded partly from our experience of people in the past, and partly also from our needs and hopes of people in the future.

In the therapeutic situation, the more disturbed and isolated the patient, the more "parental" will his projections upon the therapist tend to be. It has so far been assumed that neurosis is a state of inner disharmony which reflects a disorder of interpersonal relationships; and that this disorder can ultimately be traced to a failure of relationship between the child and his parents. It has already been pointed out, and may here be emphasized, that this is not a simple matter of blaming the parents for everything that goes wrong with the child's development, but of an extremely complex interaction between differing personalities which is always relative, not absolute. For instance, a patient may complain of his father being restrictive and tyrannical whereas the father might affirm that, since the patient never made any attempt to stand up to him, there was little chance of his being regarded in any other light. There are always faults, and virtues, on both sides in any human situation. The more complete, however, the failure of the relationship between the child and his parents, the less will the former be able to realize his own potentialities and to make satisfactory object-relationships; and the more will he be arrested in a stage of development where every person to whom he turns for help will be regarded as a parent.

One of the most striking features of human development, as compared with that of other animals, is the long period of immaturity of the young; and it is probably this which renders man liable to neurosis as well as making possible his greatest achievements. The child is for many years bound to consider himself as feeble, and adults as powerful, and one characteristic of emotional immaturity in later life is that the subject believes himself to be comparatively weak, while regarding the object as comparatively strong.

If a person believes himself to be relatively weak and helpless, he may react to other people in either of two opposite ways. He may cling to others as affording help and protection, or he may avoid them as threatening domination and restriction. The developing child usually shows these two attitudes quite clearly. When hurt or frightened he will run to the mother for aid and comfort; but, if she threatens his independence by being overprotective or dictatorial, he will react with avoidance and anger. The child both needs objects, and fears being dominated by objects; and this is one fundamental reason for the ambivalent nature of the parent-child relationship.

In the transference situation these alternative attitudes are faithfully reproduced and, although both can be detected in every patient, it is usual for one or other to predominate. Any experienced psychotherapist will be familiar with the fact that there are two extreme types of patient who cause him particular difficulty. One type is always struggling to get closer to him, clings desperately to him, and is apparently intensely involved in the analytical situation. The other tries to keep him off, avoids any personal relationship as far as possible, and is apparently quite indifferent to his therapeutic efforts. The former behaves as if the therapist might abandon him at any moment; the latter as if the therapist perpetually threatened his separate existence.

These opposing attitudes are but one manifestation of a dichotomy which, I believe, runs right through the various types of psychiatric disorder and which is familiar under various guises in the works of many psychiatrists with very different approaches. The first attitude is characteristic of the more extraverted, the second of the more introverted personality. By far the most complete and searching description of these opposing types is to be found in Jung's *Psychological Types*. I am not here attempting to recapitulate or summarize Jung's work, but rather to examine in the light of it what I conceive to be a difference in the basic attitude to objects as it appears in the transference situation, since this throws a light on the development of object-relationships in general. Jung is more concerned with normal than with neurotic psychology, whereas, in the dichotomy which I am attempting to portray, I am specifically concerned with the persistence of childish attitudes towards objects; in other words, with psychopathology. In order to underline this, I shall call the more extraverted attitude depressive, and the more introverted attitude schizoid. Both are essentially negative attitudes based upon fear, but the type of fear is different in each case.

I have come to regard the fear of being abandoned by the object as characteristic of the types who can be described under the headings extraverted, hysterical, cycloid, manic-depressive. In contrast, the fear of being dominated by the object is the basic fear of the types characterized as introverted, obsessional, schizoid, schizophrenic. In an earlier chapter I suggested that men need relationships with each other on equal terms as whole people in order to realize their full potentialities: and I also suggested that there could be a failure to achieve such a relationship by one of the two people becoming identified with and incorporated in the other, and hence failing to maintain a separate existence. In the transference situation, owing to his initially superior position, it is unlikely that the therapist will be incorporated by the patient; but there is a danger that the patient will lose his identity in that of the therapist, and it is this which the schizoid patient principally fears. The preservation of the integrity of the personality demands that there shall be relationships with others; but essentially that these relationships shall be on equal terms.

The fear of being dominated and overwhelmed by the object results in the schizoid subjects keeping away from any close relationship, and accounts for the apparent detachment and air of superiority exhibited by schizoid persons, who give the impression that they have no need of other people, and no particular regard for them. There is considerable difficulty in both giving and receiving affection; for to the schizoid subject the establishment of affectionate ties with others is always dangerous, since it seems to put him in their power. Fairbairn, in his brilliant delineation of the schizoid character, states that one reason why the latter is unable to show affection is that he has come to believe that his love is bad and even damaging to others. I am more impressed with what might be called the paranoid side of the picture, the fear that showing affection may lead to the subject's personality being invaded or dominated. I entirely agree with the view expressed by both Jung and Fairbairn, that the values of the introverted schizoid subject are heaped up in his inner world, and that he therefore tends to undervalue the object. This is why schizoid people are apt to make an initially unpleasant impression; for we all like to feel that we are valued, and it is disconcerting to be confronted by a person who denies us this satisfaction. I have the impression, not yet confirmed, that the schizoid subject, when he is phobic, is more likely to be claustrophobic than agoraphobic, in accordance with his tendency to fear and resent restriction. In the course of treatment it is easy for the therapist to underestimate the patient's progress; and he may sometimes be surprised to hear from relatives or friends how much improvement he is showing. The projection upon the therapist which constitutes the negative aspect of the transference will be that of a parent who is liable to dominate, to overwhelm, and ultimately to destroy the patient: and the patient's progress will be dependent upon the extent to which this projection can be withdrawn. The principal danger of the schizoid subject is that he becomes so isolated from other people that his development as an individual cannot proceed.

The fear of being abandoned by the object leads to the depressive subject clinging to people at all costs. Above all, he is frightened of being left alone—and hence he becomes easily emotionally involved with others and tends to identify himself too closely with them. His chief difficulty is in showing any aggression towards his fellows, for they always have to be placated in order that they may not abandon him (it has already been pointed out that a certain aggressiveness is necessary for the maintenance of a separate existence as a personality). The object tends to be overvalued, and the subject undervalued, with the consequent danger that the subject may come to feel himself worthless and thus become dangerously depressed. (In this regard it is worth repeating the clinical observation which has been frequently made that patients recovering from an attack of depression tend to become aggressive to those who are looking after them.) Since the object is overvalued, the subject tends to make a pleasant first impression. If he is phobic, he seems more likely to suffer from agoraphobia than claustrophobia, since he fears being left alone in an empty space more than being cribbed, cabined, and confined. In the course of treatment, it is easy for the therapist to overestimate the patient's progress owing to the latter's anxiety to please him. The projection upon the therapist which constitutes the negative aspect of the transference will be that of a parent who is liable to withdraw support, to disappear, and to abandon the subject; and the patient's progress will be dependent upon the extent to which this projection can be withdrawn. The principal danger of the depressive subject is that he becomes lost as a personality, in that his dependence leads to an over-identification with the object, with the result that he disappears as a separate entity.

It will be observed that the schizoid subject fears being overwhelmed, and so tends to become isolated; whereas the depressive subject fears being isolated and so may become overwhelmed.

These fundamental attitudes towards objects are reflected in the patient's relationship with the therapist, which in the initial stages of treatment is bound to be in some respects a repetition of his relationship with his parents. It has been assumed that, if that earlier relationship had been perfect, the subject would have developed in an ideal fashion, and hence would not be presenting himself for treatment; and it follows from this that these transference projections upon the therapist are essentially negative. To put this in a different way, the patient must have had "bad" parents, at least relatively to himself, or he would not be a patient; and, since he is bound to be conditioned by his past, he is equally bound to project images of such parents upon the therapist.

As the therapeutic situation develops it is hoped that the patient will come to realize, through repeated emotional experiences, that it is possible for him to have a relationship with a parental figure in which he is accepted as he is, and in which he is safe from the dangers outlined above. The negative parental projection will be withdrawn in so far as this new relationship with the analyst becomes established; and it is by means of this process that the patient comes to accept himself as he is. As Fairbairn[2] states:

> It is the patient's relationship to the analyst that mediates the "curing" or "saving" effect of psychotherapy. Where long-term psycho-analytical treatment is concerned, what mediates the "curing" or "saving" process more specifically is the development of the patient's relationship to the analyst, through a phase in which earlier pathogenic relationships are repeated under the influence of transference, into a new kind of relationship which is at once satisfying and adapted to the circumstances of outer reality.

The gradual discovery that the therapist is genuinely able to accept the patient as he is enables the latter to resolve the negative transference, and to regard the therapist as a "good" rather than a "bad" parent. It might be considered that this still leaves the patient in a state of immaturity, since he is still theoretically related to the therapist as child to parent. In practice, since it is precisely the lack of this "good" relationship with the parent which has led to the dissociation of the patient's personality, and laid the foundations of his neurosis, it is usual to find that the patient does not remain in the dependent position, and that his growth towards maturity proceeds *pari passu* with the development of his new relationship to the therapist. This generally becomes less parental, in accordance with the idea previously advanced, that a good parent is essentially a parent who can encourage and tolerate separation.

It might be concluded from what has been said that the

whole of the therapeutic process consisted in the withdrawal of negative projections from the therapist. If this
were so, therapy would be impossible, for there would be
no reason for the patient to continue in a situation which
was nothing but a repetition of the past. Positive images of
"good" parents are also projected upon the analyst, and it
seems probable that these images have two sources. First, it
can confidently be asserted that no parent is wholly "bad,"
and that, however distorted the patient's early experience
may have been, he will probably have retained some impression of what it is like to have a good parent by whom
he felt accepted, even though his conscious recollection
may deny this. Second, it seems highly probable that Jung
is right in regarding the psyche as self-regulating; and there
will thus be a tendency for people to imagine and to seek
out what has been missing in their own development just
as animals deprived of salt will travel miles to find a salt-
lick. A practical demonstration of this was afforded me by
a visit to an orphanage where the majority of the children
could not remember their mothers, and in most instances
did not know who they were. I was told that, in spite of
this, all the children had invented mothers, whose existence was usually substantiated with a wealth of fantasy. In
the case of patients whose early relationships have been
very much disturbed or absent, it is not unusual to see a
compulsive search for the missing parent, whose image may
be projected upon many different people, including the
therapist; and I take this to be a compensatory activity of
the psyche to remedy its own deficiency. This type of projection is comparable to that already described as occurring
in pre-adolescence, when the child seeks out and idealizes
people whom it needs for its own development.

The degree to which the patient regards himself as

weak, and the therapist as powerful, is one measure of the severity of the patient's failure to mature: the degree to which he regards the therapist as wholly "good" or wholly "bad" is another.

Those with experience in the analysis of psychotic patients will recognize that it is such patients (contrary to Freud's original expectation) who exhibit the most intense transference, and that this is extremely unstable in that alterations in the picture of the therapist may occur with bewildering rapidity. All transference relationships are necessarily ambivalent, just as it is inevitable that a child's relationship to its parents is ambivalent: but it is characteristic of the transference formed by the most severely disturbed patients that there can be a sudden alternation between the extremes of positive and negative, so that on one occasion the therapist is treated as a god, and on another as a devil.

These incompatible images reflect the hopes of the patient on the one hand, and his fears on the other: and are clearly derived from early childhood, when a parent was "good" in so far as he gratified the child's wishes, and "bad" in so far as he frustrated them. In a phase when the therapist is regarded as bad, the patient will often break off treatment or threaten suicide, only to return at a later stage demanding an increased number of appointments and affirming the absolute necessity of seeing the therapist as frequently as possible. This type of transference indicates a failure to develop beyond a primitive stage of infantile dependence in which, as I have already attempted to describe, people are regarded entirely from the subjective point of view and not at all as separate entities in their own right: and patients at this stage may require the additional support and freedom from the problems of daily life which can be given by admitting them to hospital.

The images projected upon the therapist by such patients are extremely primitive and, as I have implied above, are more like personifications of good and evil than any actual human being. No human mother is so wise, so understanding, and so beneficent as the Mother of God: nor could any mortal woman be as vengeful, as demanding, and as destructive as Kali. These images of the good and evil mother can be found all over the world in various forms; and it is this kind of fact which led Jung to advance his theory of archetypes. Psycho-analysis, stressing the helplessness of the infant, and the necessarily solipsistic view which it must have of objects, conceives that these primitive images originate in actual pathogenic experiences of infancy and become established as "internal objects" in the infant psyche. Analytical psychology, on the other hand, would regard such images as archetypal, as underlying the normal experience which any infant has of its mother, and would only consider their continued projection in adult life as pathological.

It does not seem to me of paramount importance, at any rate in the practice of psychotherapy, whether one believes such phenomena to be the result of very early events in the life of the infant or as the expression of inborn characteristics of the human psyche. What is important is the recognition that the projection of these images is an indication of a lack of any real relationship with the person who carries the projection. Actual people are neither gods nor devils, but human beings who are neither so powerful for good nor for evil as these terms imply; and it is only when we have no real contact with another person that we can project upon them so wholeheartedly. In war-time, when the majority of people feel at the mercy rather than in control of events, there is a general regression to a more childish condition in which projections of this kind are almost universal. The enemy, blackened by propaganda, become devilish, whereas the leader of one's own side can do no wrong. But the enemy will remain wholly evil only so long as there is no fraternization with them; and the saviour of his people had better keep aloof from them if he wishes to preserve his moral superiority. Professor Cohn,[3] in *The Pursuit of the Millennium*, has demonstrated that misery and social disintegration evoke a collective tendency to seek a saviour who will lead his people to millenniary bliss: and, whereas the saviour and his followers are wholly good, those who oppose him are wholly bad. This is, as the author indicates, a paranoid system on a mass scale.

Just as the collective phenomenon springs from misery and social disintegration, so the personal manifestation of it in the transference situation demonstrates the patient's profound isolation and lack of any adult contact with others.

But the therapeutic relationship is one which does not wholly consist of projections: it is also a relationship between two people which is taking place here and now. A relationship based entirely on projection is psychotic, and therefore no relationship at all: and I cannot agree with the popular conception that the therapist is merely a blank screen upon whom the patient can project his fantasies. The question of whether the relationship between patient and therapist is a real one, or whether the therapist's apparent concern for the patient is simply assumed for the purpose of therapy, is often raised, especially by patients who have never been able to trust anyone and who feel threatened by an offer to help. So far as I am able to judge from my own experience, I would say that for the therapist to care for his patient in a genuine way is the best possible basis for treatment. Caring for another person in an objective way is, I believe, both possible and desirable, and is entirely different from being involved with them emotionally in a subjective fashion. If the therapist is so involved, either by projecting upon his patient or by identifying with him, he may be described as exhibiting counter-transference.

If a child is to develop satisfactorily as an individual in his own right, it is necessary that his parents should not have a vested interest in him. Parents who identify themselves with their children and demand that the children shall be as like themselves as possible are simply loving themselves narcissistically, not the children. Parents who demand that the children shall be different from themselves in the sense of achieving more, or being better than themselves, are projecting into the children their own unrealized potentialities and, by living vicariously in the children, are failing to regard them as separate entities. Love based on projection and identification is ultimately self-love, not love which speeds growth and differentiation. The parent needs to love his children objectively if they are to develop happily: the psychotherapist should have a similar attitude to his patients if they are to become more mature. In other words, the psychotherapist needs to be free from counter-transference.

The essential feature of counter-transference is that the patient becomes of emotional importance to the therapist in a subjective rather than in an objective way. I have already expressed the belief that the therapist needs to care for his patients in a genuine fashion. We all have our limitations, and no one can like or care for every patient who comes to consult him. Where long-term psychotherapy is concerned, a trial period will usually reveal whether or not there is likely to be any insurmountable incompatibility. Psychotherapists must be able to care for their patients; but there is a world of difference between caring for someone and becoming emotionally involved with them. What are the ways in which counter-transference can show itself?

Perhaps the commonest difficulty is for the therapist to identify himself with his patient. This is especially likely to happen with patients who are temperamentally similar to himself, or who happen to have the same kind of emotional problems from which he himself has suffered. If this occurs the patient will lack any real relationship with the therapist, for the latter, though intensely sympathetic with him, is bound to fail to provide that degree of difference from the patient without which the latter cannot discover himself as a separate entity. A bond of identity is a bond of mutual unconsciousness—an interaction in which two people simply reflect each other and support each other, but in which no development is possible, since there is not sufficient differentiation for either to become more aware of his separate identity.

A second type of difficulty is that in which the therapist projects some unrealized part of himself into the patient. He then becomes too anxious that the patient shall fulfil what he himself has been unable to achieve. Most people, including psychotherapists, have unrealized potentialities, or feel that *if only* (fatal phrase) their course in life had been slightly different they themselves would have been different, or would have achieved a greater success in some field other than that which they have chosen. It is easy for the psychotherapist to become fascinated by aspects of the patient's personality which are in fact unrealized parts of his own: and thus to try and steer the patient in a direction which properly belongs to his own personality and not to that of the patient.

Falling in love with the patient is a danger of which most psychotherapists are well aware, but to which they nevertheless occasionally succumb. Such a misfortune is fatal to the progress of treatment since, owing to the nature of the therapeutic relationship, a sexual bond between therapist and patient is bound to be incestuous, and to interfere with the development of the patient's personality in precisely the same way as we have already indicated that parent-child incest is liable to do.

More subtle is the danger that the psychotherapist will use the patient to bolster his own self-esteem, and treat him as someone to show off to, or even to dominate. If the therapist has ideas of his own, he may use the patient as a proof of a theory and encourage the production of interesting psychopathological material which he can use for writing papers and books. Occasionally a psychotherapist may be a fanatic who wishes to convert his patient to a particular philosophy or set of beliefs, and thus to indoctrinate him, rather than encourage him to find his own way and construct his own philosophy of life. This possibility is discussed in the next chapter.

It is desirable, however, for psychotherapists to be conscious of, and prepared to state, their fundamental beliefs. Since a man's convictions are bound to affect his conduct and his attitude towards others, it is possible for a patient to be influenced by the beliefs of the psychotherapist, even though these have never been explicitly stated. Moreover, there may be a stage at which it is necessary for the psychotherapist to say quite openly what he believes in order that the patient may be able to reach a further stage of differentiation. One cannot differentiate oneself from an enigma; and, although I am convinced of the necessity of the therapist keeping himself entirely in the background during nearly all the time he spends in therapy, I also recognize that there are times when he may have to reveal more of himself in order that the patient can make further progress.

CHAPTER 12

PSYCHOTHERAPY AND INDOCTRINATION

*But the power of instruction is seldom of much efficacy,
except in those happy dispositions where it is largely
superfluous.*   GIBBON[1]

It has been suggested above that the efficacy of analytical
psychotherapy depends upon the development of the relationship between the therapist and his patient; and that
the degree of therapeutic success is proportional to the degree of maturity attained in this relationship. A mature relationship has already been defined as one in which neither
submits to or dominates the other; in which each treats the
other as a whole person in his own right; and in which
each accepts and respects his differences from the other. If
this hypothesis is correct, it follows that such therapeutic
success as may be obtained does not depend upon the acceptance by the patient of the therapist's convictions, but
rather upon the patient reaching a stage of development in
which he feels free to make up his own mind and to reach
his own convictions.

This is not to imply that the therapist should himself
have no convictions, even if this were possible; for he would
then be a nonentity with whom no one could make a relationship. It is indeed important that the therapist should
have a point of view of his own and that he should be as

aware of it as possible; for only so can he be a personality in his own right to whom the patient can relate.

But the fact that the therapist holds a certain point of view does not mean that this particular way of looking at life has to be implanted within the patient for therapeutic success to be achieved; and it is actually a sign of failure if the patient emerges from the analytical situation merely echoing the psychotherapist's opinions. If psychotherapy is successful, it encourages people to be more themselves as independent entities and, therefore, to find their own way of life in terms of their own inherited dispositions. The idea of indoctrination, of implanting dogmatic beliefs, is, or should be, entirely foreign to the spirit of any form of analytical psychotherapy.

Nevertheless, some psychiatrists have compared the analytical process to a conversion experience, and have supposed that such effectiveness as they concede it to possess depends upon the indoctrination of the patient with a set of dogmas derived from the analytical school to which the psychotherapist happens to adhere. In other words, they suggest that a successfully treated patient is a convert to a religion; and that the therapist must be a fervent believer, intent on acquiring proselytes, who desires nothing so much as to imbue his patients with his own dogmatic beliefs.

Is analytical psychotherapy really brain-washing of a more humane variety? By exposing patients to the therapeutic relationship, are we in fact depriving them of their individuality, putting our own ideas into their minds, converting them? The indoctrinator tries, by force if necessary, to compel his victim to accept a dogma and to convert him to a different way of life. Is the psychotherapist, however well-intentioned, pursuing the same path and achieving by kindlier means that conversion which the indoctrinator attempts to ensure by forceful persuasion? If so, we had better drop our attempts at analysis. It is surely better that people should be allowed to continue in neurotic misery than that they should have their freedom interfered with to this extent.

It is obvious that, however detached the therapist tries to be, he cannot avoid influencing his patient. Even if he is scrupulous in eschewing the use of direct suggestion, his attitude to life, the kind of person he himself is, will be communicated to the patient however carefully he tries not to obtrude his own personality. The popular picture of the analyst as a completely impersonal interpreter of behaviour, who is simply a blank screen upon whom the patient can project images of people from his past, is not one which can be sustained in reality. There is also an actual relationship between patient and therapist at the time of meeting; and there can be no actual relationship between human beings without mutual influence.

Indoctrination, however, unlike analytical psychotherapy, is not a matter of mutual influence but of the complete domination of one person by another. It presupposes an authority who is in possession of "the truth" on the one hand and a more or less misguided victim on the other, who, like the guests of Procrustes, is forced to conform to a rigid structure which is unlikely to fit him exactly. Indoctrination is didactic, coercive, and authoritarian. It is, therefore, entirely opposed to the kind of development of the individual personality which, I have suggested, is the aim of analytical psychotherapy.

Although I do not believe that the psychotherapeutic process depends upon or should involve indoctrination, there is some excuse for those who, knowing little of analytical methods, have advanced such a view: for the behaviour of certain analysts on the one hand, and certain patients on the other, might be thought to imply it. The tendency of psychotherapists to form esoteric groups has already been admitted, and deplored, in an earlier part of this book: and it is true that some analysts resemble converts to a religion whose lives are enthralled by their faith to the exclusion of any other activity. Such are the analysts who are unable to communicate effectively with anyone who is not of their persuasion; who insist on their own children being analysed from an early age; who are themselves permanently "in analysis" with one or other of their colleagues; and who, after spending ten or more hours of the day treating patients, seem unable to find any more agreeable way of spending an evening than by attending an analytical meeting.

Behaviour of this kind is likely to give rise to the idea that those who practise any form of analytical psychotherapy are fanatics intent on forcing their patients to accept doctrinaire assertions. Nevertheless, there is no evidence that I know of to support the hypothesis that patients who have been treated by even the most fanatical of analysts necessarily continue to subscribe to the particular views either of the therapist who has treated them or of the school to which the latter belongs. Amongst psychotherapists themselves there is certainly a tendency to form esoteric groups; but the number and variety of such groups, and the frequent disagreements both within and between them, do not suggest that dogmas are handed down unchanged from generation to generation as they are in some religious and political sects. The very fact that there are so many splinter groups within the various analytical schools may be thought to imply that the analytical process leads not to uniformity but to a greater diversity of belief. "*Quot homines, tot sen-*

tentiae" is an aphorism which is confirmed rather than undermined by psychotherapy: and common ground between different groups of analysts is to be found, not in their theoretical assumptions, but in their attitude to the individual.

It is not only the behaviour of certain therapists which gives rise to the suspicion that analysis is a process of indoctrination: some patients also may give the impression of having been indoctrinated, at any rate temporarily. In the last chapter it was pointed out that there were two extreme types of patient who could be distinguished by their attitude to the therapist: those whose basic fear was of being abandoned, and those whose principal dread was of being overwhelmed. These two fears seem to be present to some extent in all men, although one may be, and usually is, far more in evidence than the other. Their existence accords well with the hypothesis already presented, that the satisfactory development of personality requires that the individual shall have relationships with other individuals, but that these relationships need to be of a kind which allows his assertion of his uniqueness.

In general it is true to say that the more extraverted patient generally has a fair number of contacts with other people; and, although these may be of a rather superficial kind, they at least protect him from complete isolation. Such people are liable to identify themselves with the therapist and thus, for a time, adopt his point of view as if it were their own: but the fact that there are other people of emotional importance in their lives dilutes the effect of this identification and makes the resolution of the positive transference comparatively easy. The more introverted patient is isolated, but not as a rule markedly dependent; and so is not generally in much danger of over-identification with the therapist or of taking over his beliefs wholesale.

But there are a few patients who exhibit both characteristics in profound measure, who are both extremely isolated and extremely dependent. Such people, because of their isolation, find in the therapist the only person who means anything to them. At the same time their dependence makes them identify with him and hang on his every word. Sometimes they alternate between trying to get as close as possible to the therapist for fear that he will abandon them, and withdrawing as far as they can for fear of being crushed by him. Such patients seem to be those who have never had any secure relationship with either parent, or indeed with any human being; and to them, for a time, the therapeutic situation is all-important, just as for the infant at the beginning of life the relationship to the mother is vital.

It is probable that this small group of patients do become temporarily indoctrinated, in the sense of identifying themselves with the analyst's ideas, in the same way that a small child at first adopts the standards and takes over the beliefs of its parents: but, if treatment proceeds satisfactorily, this phase will pass, for the patient will extend and deepen his relationship with other people, and also lose his fear of differing from the therapist, just as a child who is secure becomes less and less afraid of differing from its parents. Not all such patients are curable, and some may go on indefinitely looking for what has been missing in their early development. It is, I believe, this group who may, in default of achieving any real relationship with another person, hold on to Jungian or Freudian or any other variety of psychological theory as if it were a dogmatic faith; and thus give rise to the impression (since it is they who talk most about it) that the analytical process is one of indoctrination.

Since the Americans became disturbed at the high proportion of men who collaborated in some way or other with the enemy while imprisoned in Korea, Communist methods of indoctrination have been exhaustively studied. The results of these studies are actually reassuring to the psychotherapist who is alarmed at the thought that he may be indoctrinating his patients rather than aiding their development as individuals. The figures show that it is not difficult, under appalling conditions, by the threat of torture or the promise of alleviation, to persuade some men who are unprepared for this treatment to collaborate with the enemy to the extent of signing peace pledges and the like. But, contrary to popular supposition, it is far from easy to produce a permanent change in a man's beliefs or to convert him to an alien point of view.

There is evidence that even those Americans who were forced to make the statements that the U.S.A. was using germ warfare did not believe what they were saying: and, in a study of these men, Winokur[2] concluded that the subjects knew that they were making false statements, but "the guilt which was aroused by the making of the statements was handled by the mechanism of rationalization in which the subjects questioned whether telling lies to the enemy could be harmful to their own country."

Less than five per cent of the soldiers exposed to Communist indoctrination in prison camps in Korea came back convinced Communists; and, of these, a number were known to be sympathetic to Communism before going to Korea, and a number have probably reverted to their previous way of thinking since their return. Both the Americans and the British agree that the indoctrination programme in Korea was ineffective in producing converts to Communism.

However, the cases which have caused most concern are those of men who made spectacular confessions of guilt in the Russia treason trials, and also those of the prisoners who emerged from Chinese prisons singing the praises of their captors. It is these cases which have given rise to the fear that there exists some infallible method of "brain-washing," of extracting one set of ideas from a man's head and replacing them with another.

In fact, it is only a very small minority even of important political prisoners who are deemed fit to appear at public trials in Russia. Hinkle and Wolff,[3] in their admirable study of Communist methods, point out that there are many reasons why a prisoner should sign a confession and repeat it in court. He may think that no one will believe it in any case, or that he will be released and can then repudiate his confession. There are even "instances of prisoners who signed depositions largely out of sympathy for their interrogators because they felt that they would be punished if a proper deposition were not forthcoming." The same authors have made a study of those who, after prolonged detention in Chinese prisons, have emerged saying that their imprisonment was deserved and a valuable experience, and who thus appear to have been thoroughly indoctrinated. It is now known that such people form a small and special group described as emotionally rootless. They were all people in rebellion against their parents and the way of life of the segment of society to which their parents belonged. They all spoke Chinese and were anxious to remain in China: and they were familiar with Marxism already, even if not actually members of "fellow-traveller" groups. Hinkle and Wolff conclude: "Thus it is quite erroneous to think that those who have experienced prison indoctrination in Communist China emerge as thoroughly indoctrinated

Communists who express praise and admiration for their captors. Such people are as unusual as the public confessors in Russian purge trials."

It may be that the small percentage of people who are converted by Communist indoctrination have much in common with the patients described above as showing both extreme isolation and extreme dependence. To determine this would require further research; but the two groups certainly share one characteristic feature—the lack of any strong attachments in their past lives.

It must come as a relief to everyone who values the freedom of the individual to know that, although a man can be temporarily broken, compelled to tell lies, or so stupefied that he cannot distinguish truth from falsehood, yet, if he returns to a normal environment, he will almost certainly recover his judgement, come back to himself, and once again be free to form his own conclusions and choose his own way of life. A study of the literature of indoctrination induces the realization that the toughness and powers of recovery of the human psyche are even more remarkable than had been supposed; and the contemplation of so much horror is relieved by the vision of such resilience.

It is certainly possible that those who undergo analytical psychotherapy become imbued with a kind of liberal humanism—for example, with the idea, implicit in any psychotherapeutic procedure, that the individual is important; or with the belief that love is better than hate, or freedom than tyranny. They may even be indoctrinated with the notion that indoctrination is an unwarrantable infringement of human liberty. But it seems highly unlikely that more than a very small proportion of patients become devoted "Freudians," or "Jungians," or "Kleinians," and any who do must be accounted therapeutic failures. Conversion is certainly a subject of psychological interest; but as a method of treatment it has nothing to commend it to the psychotherapist. In fact, the total acceptance of a creed which was previously unacceptable must arouse his suspicions. The reversal of a man's basic tenets argues a certain instability, and it can never be certain that a further reversal to the original condition will not occur. It is those who exhibit fanaticism and dogmatism who are most likely to switch their allegiance, just as it is those who exhibit the most powerful feelings in the transference situation who most easily reverse their picture of the analyst.

Dogmatism and fanaticism are signs of an inner disharmony of personality, of a precarious adjustment which is the very opposite of the calm acceptance of his own beliefs and those of others which characterizes the man who is at peace with himself. Maturity requires that a man shall know his own mind and be aware of his own convictions; but the more he achieves the realization of his own personality the less bigoted will he generally become.

CHAPTER 13

THE INTEGRITY OF
THE PERSONALITY

*The greatest thing in the world is to know how to belong
to ourselves.* MONTAIGNE[1]

I believe that each human being, in spite of sharing many
characteristics with his fellows, is genetically endowed with
a unique personality. Just as all living things grow, develop,
and come to be whatever their inherited structure prede-
termines that they shall be, so a man is urged on by forces
of which he may be largely unconscious to express his own
uniqueness, to be himself, to realize his own personality.
That it is genetic variation which is ultimately responsible
for differences in personality seems certain; for, although
what is inherited and how remains obscure, the differences
are too wide to be accounted for by environment alone.

It has already been pointed out that it is the long period
of men's immaturity compared with that of other animals
which makes possible the achievements of civilization; for
a prolonged immaturity implies a continuing plasticity and
an extended capacity to learn. His large brain makes possible the complexity of man's psychic structure, and his
partial emancipation from the tyranny of instinct is dependent upon this complexity. For, although the broad outlines
of his behaviour are laid down and he can never escape
from the confines of his biological endowment, man is less

bound by rigid instinctual patterns than any other animal. The fundamental, archetypal themes are common to all men; the individual variations upon these themes are apparently indefinite. A bird or insect is rigidly confined, and instinct compels it to do exactly the same things in the same way. The relative simplicity of the nervous system enforces stereotypy of behaviour; and so birds and insects of the same species are practically indistinguishable from each other. Men, on the other hand, though sharing the same basic instincts, because of their complexity, express these instincts in varying, indirect, and subtle ways; and so exhibit that differentiation from each other which we call personality. Although in the species as a whole the possibilities of variation are infinite, in the individual they are limited by inheritance. No one can tell what sort of a person a baby will become; but within it a mysterious process is continuing which will lead to its becoming itself alone; to the emergence of a new, a unique individual. Something within the human ovum determines that it will develop into a human foetus and nothing else; it seems that there is a similar pre-formed organization independent of consciousness which is struggling to emerge and which will ultimately manifest itself as the mature personality.

But the protracted immaturity of the human child means that, for many years, he is weak and helpless and consequently liable to influence. He needs, above all, the security of an objective love which is unconditional, a love which, by accepting him as he is, enables him to become himself in the full flower of his individuality. If such love were unequivocally available, perhaps his development could proceed without hindrance and his mature personality emerge without conflict and without distortion. But no child is ever so fortunate; and some deflection from its own true path is therefore inevitable, however benevolent his parents and however robust his own nature. The complexity of his psychic structure makes possible dissociation and repression; his helplessness ensures his conformity, and so a condition is created in which parts of his personality are denied expression and he becomes, and may remain, something less than fully himself. "There is no one whose libidinal development proceeds wholly without a hitch"; and we are all partially neurotic, all, in some degree, less than entirely ourselves.

The difference between people who are sufficiently neurotic to seek, or to need, psychotherapeutic help, and that mysterious being the "normal" man is one of degree, not of kind; and there can be no one who has not at times suffered from the inner disharmony which gives rise to neurotic symptoms. To be neurotic is to suffer from intrapsychic conflict. It is a subjective state manifesting itself in subjective symptoms of which none but the victim may be aware. The existence of a severe degree of neurosis does not preclude considerable success, in the sense of conventional achievement; in fact, certain types of success can probably not be attained without a compulsive drive for power which most psychiatrists would regard as pathological. There is no correlation between neurosis and intelligence, nor between neurosis and practical effectiveness. There are many ineffective people in the world who are not neurotic, just as there are many neurotics who are far from ineffective. But inquiry into the interpersonal relationships of neurotics reveals a lack of maturity, a failure to progress beyond a childish preoccupation with being worse than, or better than, others; an inability to love and be lovable; a failure to achieve that relationship of whole person to whole person which is the outward sign of an inward integration.

"Neurotics are persons whose real actions are blocked."[2]
In other words, they are people whose personalities are only
partially manifested, and neurotic symptoms are essentially
due to a conflict between the attempted emergence of the
true individual and the fears which forbid this emergence.
No child can conceivably have an ideally smooth development; but, if things go reasonably well, he will, as he gets
older, gradually discover and accept his own nature. His
increasing security and recognition of his own powers enable him to emerge from identification with his parents and
to dispense with those introjected aspects of their psychology which do not accord with his own inner nature. By
projecting upon and identifying with new people he is gradually able to disclose his own dormant potentialities, to
discover his own personality, and to correct such divaga-
tions from his own path as have been imposed upon his
immaturity. The degree to which this process of self-
realization is completed determines the degree of neurosis
in adult life.

We know that all children need that love which I have
called objective if they are to develop satisfactorily: but we
are far from understanding all the complexities of the interaction between heredity and environment which determines how much difficulty the individual may encounter in
realizing his own personality. In spite of the work of such
men as Kretschmer and Sheldon, in spite of the typology
of Jung and the researches of the geneticists, we have as yet
no reliable yardstick of innate human differences, no
knowledge which would enable us to predict and make pro-
vision for the differing requirements of different temperamental endowments. Parents and children may be very
variously constituted; but, if there obtains between them a
love which accepts and welcomes differences, the majority

of emotional difficulties will be solved in the course of the child's development; and such parts of his personality as fail to emerge or are disowned within the home will be evoked by the contacts he makes outside it. If, however, the child has become sufficiently disturbed for it to be difficult for him to form new attachments, a condition of neurosis which is not outgrown may persist.

It is at this point that the psychotherapist may prove of value. If he is adequately trained, he should be able to accept and make contact with a wider range of personalities than the average person. Moreover, the fact that psychotherapy is his chosen profession renders tolerable and even exciting the adventure of attempting to make a relationship with someone whose own efforts in this regard have failed, and who is therefore unable to progress in his own development. One cannot foretell how far any individual will be able to progress towards his own maturity; but the psychotherapist, if he is sufficiently at peace with himself, can at least provide the background of emotional security against which further development is possible; and this is, I believe, his essential function. The technique he employs, the views which he holds, are probably of comparatively little importance; the attitude he has to the patient and the relationship he makes with him are vital.

Is it possible for a man ever to belong to himself, as Montaigne expresses it; to know who he is, to be no less, and to strive to be no more, than his endowment demands of him? Jung says,[3] "Personality is the supreme realization of the innate idiosyncrasy of a living being. It is an act of high courage flung in the face of life, the absolute affirmation of all that constitutes the individual, the most successful adaptation to the universal conditions of existence coupled with the greatest possible freedom for self-determination." These are fine words; but are they any more than that? Can a man ever really achieve unity and wholeness; or are we simply spinning empty phrases, toying with phantom ideals, which may arouse our ardour without affecting our behaviour? I do not believe that anyone ever reaches a condition of complete inner harmony; but those who seem to approach most nearly to this ideal share certain attributes. Jung says:[4] "There is no personality without definiteness, wholeness, and ripeness": and to these characteristics one might add consistency, freedom from compulsion, and maturity of interpersonal relationships. People whose public and private lives are widely discrepant can hardly be said to be integrated; and maturity demands that the personality shall be recognizably the same under varying circumstances. The sense of compulsion, of being driven by an alien force, which attends neurotic striving for power and neurotic sexuality, disappears when a man is able to realize his own powers and to express his sexuality. To achieve the best one is capable of is to be freed from the compulsion to do "better than": to be able to give and to receive love in a mature relationship is to be freed from compulsive sexuality.

We are both limited and free, and we can never escape from our instincts, which must, therefore, find expression; but we attain the greatest freedom when we recognize our limitations. If we do not strive to be superior to, we shall not be dominated by, our instinctive dispositions. That the achievement of personality is characterized by maturity of interpersonal relationships is a principal theme of this book; and the man who is icily remote from, or slavishly dependent upon, his fellows cannot be regarded as having reached his full stature as a human being. But, however detailed our observation, we cannot from outside comprehend what is essentially an inner experience. I have been at pains to point out that neurosis is a subjective state, and that, although certain aspects of a person's behaviour may enable one to deduce an inner disturbance, only the subject himself can know the extent to which he is riven by conflict. Similarly, the sense of being at one with oneself, of being true to and in harmony with one's own nature, is ultimately a subjective experience; and, although we may think that we can recognize when a man has attained this condition, it is really only the individual himself who knows his own truth.

At the beginning of this chapter I postulated a pre-formed organization independent of consciousness which in the child is struggling to emerge, and which in the adult will ultimately manifest itself as the mature personality. Some such working hypothesis seems inescapable, since it is clear that consciousness can never comprehend the whole person. Part of the human condition is that we can never know ourselves completely; for we are both observer and observed and must, therefore, in some degree perpetually elude our own surveillance. However much insight we have, we can never see the whole of ourselves, never be conscious of the totality of our being. It cannot therefore be consciousness alone which directs the course of the individual towards his own maturity; and, indeed, it would be surprising if it were, since other living things grow, develop, and live out their lives without showing much evidence of possessing consciousness in the human sense at all.

The subjective sense of being at one with oneself, of possessing that inner serenity which stands at the opposite pole to neurosis, is, in fact, often accompanied by a feeling that there is something superior to the ego, something which is, as it were, directing the course of the individual's development and to which it behoves him to pay attention. If such phrases as "personal integrity," "fidelity to the law of one's own being," being "true to oneself" are anything more than catchwords, one is bound to postulate some totality of the personality which is greater than that ego with which we habitually identify ourselves; for, if a man can be either true or untrue to himself, the self to which he is either true or untrue cannot be identical with that executive part of him to which these epithets apply. Readers of Jung will recognize his concept of a self, superior to the ego, which represents the individual in his totality, not simply that aspect of himself of which he happens to be conscious.

Those to whom such a concept is strange, or initially uncongenial, may perhaps be more prepared to entertain it when they recall that we often use such ideas in another context. A work of art such as a novel or a symphony is, if of high calibre, often referred to as possessing the qualities of inner coherence and inevitability. We feel that only this phrase could have followed that; that this incident, and no other, could appear at a particular point, that only thus could the work be ended. There is, it appears, an organization or inner structural pattern which somehow embraces the work as a whole and is superior to its individual phrases; and it is partly this sense of the whole being greater than the sum of its parts which excites our admiration. The numerous descriptions of the creative process afforded us by artists of all kinds, and indeed by scientists also, amply attest the fact that the artist himself is often unaware of how his creation will finally manifest itself, and may be surprised to find how surely its end is foreshadowed in its beginning.

If, however, we admit such a hypothesis to our view of the human psyche, we are certainly inviting criticism of the most devastating kind. History can parade before us an immense number of deluded cranks who have felt themselves to be the agents of a superior force, and who have justified their most abominable actions by placing the responsibility for them on God, on Fate, or on some lesser luminary by whom they believed themselves to be guided or inspired. Aldous Huxley,[5] in his brilliant essay "Justifications," tells us of the Swiss Anabaptist, Thomas Schucker, who, commanded as he believed by the deity, cut off his brother's head with a sword in the presence of a large number of people. Was Thomas Schucker being true to himself, following the predestined path of his own development, or was he simply acting out an infantile fantasy? He himself asserted the former view; most of us would incline to the latter: but this extreme example raises an interesting problem. If we admit the hypothesis of a self to which the individual can be true, are we not inviting delusion and failing to distinguish between the maturely integrated individual and the psychotic?

Once again we meet the curious link which joins the opposite poles of the development of personality, and to which I referred in an earlier chapter. The infant is, in one sense, a whole; for, in its solipsistic isolation, it is itself, no less, no more. "Nearest then to Tao is the infant."[6] But its entire spontaneity rests upon the fact that its only relationship with people is one of total dependence, which, in the most primitive stage, is not a relationship at all, since other people are not distinguished as separate objects but treated as part of the subject. This attitude towards objects is also characteristic of the psychotic, who may be assumed to be emotionally still in an infantile stage of development; and our theoretical difficulty over such people as Thomas

Schucker may be resolved if we pay attention not to their beliefs but to their object relationships.

In the introduction I suggested that a delusion is characterized not so much by its truth or falsity as by the emotional intensity with which it is held: it is a citadel to be defended against other people, not a hypothesis which can be discussed with them. Many reasonable people hold beliefs which other reasonable people may regard as fantastic; but, provided they do not think that they alone have a monopoly of the truth and that everyone else is wrong, their sanity is not in question. Trollope[7] entitled his novel about a man's delusions *He Knew He was Right*, a title which aptly underlines the essential feature of paranoia. To *know* one is right is to disregard the beliefs of others and to fail to treat them as persons in their own right, entitled to their own views. Thomas Schucker knew that he was right, but we may doubt whether his brother would have shared his conviction if he had realized what was to happen to him. A tolerant scepticism, an ability to doubt one's own ideas as well as those of other people, is a good test of maturity: fanaticism, insanity, and an infantile attitude to others are closely related.

Self-realization, so far as anyone ever achieves it, is manifested by the widest exercise of the individual's potentialities combined with the attainment of a mature relationship with others. Subjectively, it seems to be attended by a sense of being fully adapted to, rather than attempting entirely to direct, the course of one's own development. This latter attitude is, in the wide sense in which Jung uses the word, religious: for it implies that the individual is acknowledging his ultimate dependence upon forces which may be depicted as either inside or outside himself, but which are nevertheless not of his making. The use of the word "religious" generally causes alarm to those who still adhere to the outmoded idea that there is some fundamental incompatibility between religion and science; but it will perhaps reassure them to realize that, in seeking to understand these phenomena, we do not have to postulate a deity ensconced within the psyche which directs the course of development. Shakespeare[8] could say: "There's a divinity that shapes our ends, rough-hew them how we will": the modern psychotherapist may prefer to use the terminology of cybernetics.

Physiologically the body is an enormously complicated structure which, until its final dissolution, is self-regulating. No automatic factory, no calculating machine can rival the complexity and the subtlety by which the internal environment of the body is kept constant so that each individual cell may function at its optimum efficiency. Wiener,[9] in his book *Cybernetics*, gives many examples of such self-regulating mechanisms. The control of body temperature, the regulation of heart-rate and blood-pressure, the maintenance of the hydrogen-ion concentration and the calcium content of the blood at the appropriate levels are but a few of many examples. These self-regulating devices function by means of negative feed-backs: that is to say that, when a change in the internal environment occurs in one direction, processes are set in motion which encourage a change in the opposite direction. Thus, a rise in body temperature sets off a whole series of changes which tend to lower it again: an increase in the alkalinity of the blood causes reactions to occur which encourage the excretion of alkali and the retention of acid, thus maintaining the pH within narrow limits. A perpetual oscillation is constantly taking place around an ideal state of equilibrium, a mean between opposites. This condition of homeostasis is always being sought but never quite attained, or, if temporarily achieved, is immediately departed from again, because either the external or the internal environment changes. The body may be said to "know" what is best for itself; but it is a knowledge without consciousness, and the goal of homeostasis is sought automatically without the deliberate direction of a conscious ego.

It seems probable that the psyche is similarly constituted, and that it is automatically seeking its own equilibrium. We owe to Jung the valuable hypothesis that the psyche is self-regulating. He believes that, in many instances, dreams and other manifestations of unconscious, spontaneous mental activity are attempts of the mind to correct its own errors—a hypothesis which necessarily implies a "right" state of affairs from which divergence can take place. In the practice of psychotherapy this theory is of great value in the interpretation and understanding of clinical material; and it would be possible to give many examples of how dreams, fantasies, and neurotic symptoms tend to counterbalance and correct a one-sided conscious attitude. Those who regret the divergence between academic and clinical psychology will be glad to recognize that the compensatory function of the unconscious is a hypothesis which can be tested, and one which has already been the subject of experimental investigation.[10]

I have made the assumption that each human being is endowed with a unique personality which is seeking its own realization. The hypothesis of a psyche which, like the body, is self-regulating lends support to the idea that it is possible for a man to discover his own personality and to belong to himself. Just as too wide a divergence from physiological equilibrium leads to discomfort, disease, and death; so the attempt to be what one is not, or the failure to be what one is, lead to internal conflicts, neurosis, and emotional isolation.

I believe the development of personality to be a natural process which, ideally, follows its own course to its own conclusion. But, since it is also a process which depends throughout its extent upon human relationships, it is easily interfered with. It is only if a child has experienced objective love that it becomes an adult capable of loving; and the full development of personality can only take place in a setting of adult loving and being loved. In seeking to define the fundamentals upon which the practice of psychotherapy rests, I find myself returning again and again to a belief in the integrity of the personality and the validity of human relationships. Truth has many aspects; and the limitations imposed by inheritance preclude each one of us from seeing more than a small part of it. The most that anyone can do is to be faithful to that aspect which he himself is able to see. Each of us has his own interpretation of the truth; but our very differences may link us more closely when we recognize that the man who is capable of the deepest human relationship is the man who is most surely himself.

REFERENCES

INTRODUCTION

1. Gibbon, Edward, *The Decline and Fall of the Roman Empire* (Methuen, 1897), Vol. III, p. 24.
2. Butterfield, Herbert, *Christianity and History* (G. Bell, 1949), p. 46.
3. Vallentin, Antonina, *Einstein* (Weidenfeld and Nicolson, London, 1954), p. 105.
4. Heim, A. W., *The Appraisal of Intelligence* (Methuen, 1954), p. 33.
5. Whitehead, A. N., *Science and the Modern World* (Cambridge University Press, 1928), p. 9.
6. Heisenberg, W., *The Physicist's Conception of Nature* (Hutchinson, 1958), p. 29.
7. Eddington, A. S., *The Nature of the Physical World* (Cambridge University Press, 1928), pp. 294–5.
8. Jung, C. G., and Pauli, W., *The Interpretation of Nature and the Psyche* (Routledge and Kegan Paul, 1955), pp. 151–2.
9. Huxley, Aldous, *T. H. Huxley as a Literary Man* (Macmillan, Huxley Memorial Lecture, 1932).

CHAPTER 1: SELF-REALIZATION

1. Streeter, B. H., *Reality* (Macmillan, 1935) pp. 313–14.
2. Richter, Derek (Ed.), *Perspectives in Neuropsychiatry* (H. K. Lewis and Co., 1950), p. 79.

CHAPTER 2: THE RELATIVITY OF PERSONALITY

1. Eddington, A. S., *The Nature of the Physical World* (Cambridge University Press, 1928), p. 144.
2. Russell, Bertrand, *History of Western Philosophy* (Allen and Unwin, 1955), p. 710.
3. Donne, John, "Devotions upon Emergent Occasions," from the complete poetry and selected prose, ed. John Hayward (The Nonesuch Press, 1939), p. 538.
4. Conrad, Joseph, *Nostromo* (Coll. ed. J. M. Dent, 1955), p. 497.
5. Freeman and McGhie, "The Psychopathology of Schizophrenia," *Brit. J. Med. Psychol.*, pp. 30, 187.
6. Fromm, Erich, *The Fear of Freedom* (Routledge and Kegan Paul, 1950), p. 15.
7. Woolf, Virginia, *The Common Reader* (Hogarth Press, 1925), p. 262.
8. Maclay, W. S., Guttmann, E., and Mayer-Gross, "Spontaneous Drawing as an Approach to some Problems of Psychopathology," *Proc. Roy. Soc. Med.*, 1938.

CHAPTER 3: THE MATURE RELATIONSHIP

1. Buber, Martin, *I and Thou*, transl. R. G. Smith (T. O. T. Clark, 1953), p. 28.
2. Brierley, Marjorie, *Trends in Psycho-Analysis* (Hogarth Press, 1951), pp. 192–3.

3. Jung, C. G., *Modern Man in Search of a Soul* (Kegan Paul, 1941), p. 270.

4. Fairbairn, W. Ronald D., *Psycho-Analytic Studies of the Personality* (Tavistock Publications, 1952), p. 145.

5. ibid., p. 32.

6. ibid., p. 55.

7. ibid., p. 47.

8. Fromm, Erich, *The Fear of Freedom* (Routledge and Kegan Paul, 1950), p. 228.

CHAPTER 4: THE DEVELOPMENT OF PERSONALITY

1. *Confessions of St. Augustine* (Methuen, 1929), Bk I, Ch. XX, p. 64.

2. Freud, Sigmund, *Introductory Lectures on Psycho-Analysis* (Allen and Unwin, 1943), p. 264.

3. Waley, Arthur, *The Way and Its Power* (Allen and Unwin, 1949), p. 55.

4. Freud, Sigmund, *New Introductory Lectures on Psycho-Analysis* (Hogarth Press, 1937), p. 139.

5. ibid., p. 124.

6. ibid., p. 139.

7. Freud, Sigmund, *Outline of Psycho-Analysis* (Hogarth Press, 1949), p. 7.

8. Money-Kyrle, R. E., *Psychoanalysis and Politics* (Duckworth, 1951), p. 49.

9. Fairbairn, W. Ronald D., *Psycho-Analytic Studies of the Personality* (Tavistock Publications, 1952), p. 106.

10. Fairbairn, W. Ronald D., "Observations on the Nature of Hysterical States," *Brit. J. Med. Psych.*, 1954, XXVII, p. 107.

11. The Gospel According to St. Matthew, 18, 3.

CHAPTER 5: THE EMERGENT PERSONALITY

1. Huxley, Aldous, *Proper Studies* (Chatto and Windus, 1933), p. 99.
2. Mayer-Gross, Slater, Roth, *Clinical Psychiatry* (Cassell, 1954), p. 190.
3. ibid., p. 277.
4. ibid., p. 279.
5. ibid., p. 220.
6. Freud, Sigmund, *Introductory Lectures on Psycho-Analysis* (Allen and Unwin, 1943), p. 346.
7. Sheldon, W. H., *The Varieties of Temperament* (Harper, 1942).
8. Kretschmer, Ernst, *Physique and Character* (Kegan Paul, 1936).
9. Tanner, J. M., "Physique, Character, and Disease," *The Lancet*, 1956, p. 637.

CHAPTER 6: IDENTIFICATION AND INTROJECTION

1. Bowra, C. M., *The Greek Experience* (Weidenfeld and Nicolson, 1957), p. 198.
2. Jung, C. G., *Psychological Types* (Kegan Paul, 1938), p. 551.
3. Fairbairn, W. Ronald D., *Psycho-Analytic Studies of the Personality* (Tavistock Publications, 1952), p. 47.
4. Bowley, John, *Child Care and the Growth of Love* (Penguin Books, 1957), p. 58.
5. Jung, C. G., Two Essays on Analytical Psychology (Routledge and Kegan Paul, 1953), p. 141.
6. Fromm, Erich, *The Fear of Freedom* (Routledge and Kegan Paul, 1950), p. 15.

CHAPTER 7: PROJECTION AND DISSOCIATIOIN

1. Terence, *Heauton timorumenos*, I, i, 25.
2. Jung, C. G., *The Undiscovered Self* (Routledge and Kegan Paul, 1958), pp. 77–8.

CHAPTER 8: IDENTIFICATION AND PROJECTION

1. Plato, *The Symposium*, transl. W. Hamilton (Penguin Books, 1951), p. 78.
2. Frazer, Sir James G., *The Golden Bough* (Abridged edition, Macmillan, 1922), p. 692.
3. Forster, E. M., *Two Cheers for Democracy* (Arnold, 1951), p. 24.
4. Proust, Marcel, *Remembrance of Things Past*, transl. Scott Moncrieff (Chatto and Windus, 1949), Vol. VII, p. 21.
5. ibid., p. 20.

CHAPTER 9: HETEROSEXUAL LOVE AND RELATIONSHIP

1. Song from *The Indian Queen*, words by Dryden and Howard, music by Henry Purcell.
2. Plato, *The Symposium*, transl. W. Hamilton (Penguin Books, 1951), p. 75.
3. Mead, Margaret, *Male and Female* (Gollancz, 1950).

CHAPTER 10: THE PSYCHOTHERAPEUTIC PROCESS

1. Forster, E. M., *Howards End* (Arnold, 1910), pp. 183–4.

CHAPTER 11: TRANSFERENCE AND
COUNTER-TRANSFERENCE

1. Blake, William, "The Marriage of Heaven and Hell,"
   Poetry and Prose of William Blake (Nonesuch Press, 1927),
   p. 201.
2. Fairbairn, W. Ronald D., "Observations in Defence of
   the Object-relations Theory of the Personality," *Brit. J.
   Med. Psych.*, Vol. XXVIII, p. 156, 1955.
3. Cohn, Norman, *The Pursuit of the Millennium* (Secker
   and Warburg, 1957).

CHAPTER 12: PSYCHOTHERAPY AND
INDOCTRINATION

1. Gibbon, Edward, *The Decline and Fall of the Roman Empire* (Methuen, 1897), Vol. I, p. 84.
2. Winokur, G., "The Germ Warfare Statements," *Journal
   of Nervous and Mental Disease*, 1955, Vol. 122.
3. Hinkle and Wolff, "Communist Interrogation and Indoctrination of 'Enemies of the State,' " A.M.A. *Ar-
   chives of Neurology and Psychiatry*, August 1956, Vol. 76,
   No. 2.

CHAPTER 13: THE INTEGRITY OF THE PERSONALITY

1. *The Essays of Montaigne*, trans. E. J. Trechmann (The
   Modern Library Edition, 1946), p. 206.
2. Fenichel, Otto, *The Psychoanalytic Theory of Neurosis*
   (W. W. Norton, New York, 1945), p. 50.
3. Jung, C. G., *The Development of Personality* (Routledge
   and Kegan Paul, 1954), p. 171.
4. ibid., p. 171.

5. Huxley, Aldous, *The Olive Tree and Other Essays* (Albatross Collected Edition, 1937), p. 91.

6. Waley, Arthur, *The Way and Its Power* (Allen and Unwin, 1949), p. 55.

7. Trollope, Anthony, *He Knew He was Right* (Oxford University Press, World's Classics, 1951).

8. Shakespeare, William, *Hamlet*, Act V, Sc. 2.

9. Wiener, Norbert, *Cybernetics* (Technology Press, John Wiley and Sons Inc., New York, 1948).

10. Bash, K. W., "Zur experimentellen Grundlegung der Jungschen Traumanalyse," *Schweiz. Z. Psychol. Anwend.*, 1952, II, 282–95.

INDEX